DEPARTMENT OF HEALTH

The Children Act 1989

Guidance and Regulations

Volume 7

Guardians Ad Litem and other Court Related Issues

A NEW FRAMEWORK FOR THE CARE
AND UPBRINGING OF CHILDREN

LONDON: HMSO

First published 1991
ISBN 0 11 321471 5

Preface

The guidance in this Volume is issued under section 7 of the Local Authority Social Services Act 1970. It is one in a series designed to bring to managers and practitioners an understanding of the principles of the Children Act and associated Regulations, to identify areas of change and to discuss the implications for policies, procedures and practice. It is not intended that any one Volume should be read as a discrete entity. The Children Act was conceived as a cohesive legal framework for the care and protection of children; each Volume of guidance should therefore be read in conjunction with the others in the series, and cross-references are made where appropriate.

The guidance is written as if the Children Act is currently in force, and refers in the past tense to legislation which is repealed by the Act.

Contents

CHAPTER 1 INTRODUCTION

1.1. This Volume brings together guidance, Regulations and other material on those aspects of the Children Act which relate to the courts. It is complementary to and should be read in conjunction with Volume 1 in this series (Court Orders).

1.2. Chapters 2–6 provide guidance for local authorities, although the material in Chapter 3 (Education Supervision Orders), prepared by the Department of Education and Science, bears mainly on local education authorities rather than social services departments. Chapter 7 includes ancillary material on the Criminal Justice Act 1991 which will have implications for the way local authorities exercise their responsibilities under the Children Act.

1.3. The Annexes reproduce the Statutory Instruments associated with the chapters of guidance, and the Emergency Protection Order (Transfer of Responsibilities) Regulations 1991, guidance on which is included in Volume 1 (Court Orders) at paragraphs 4.32 and 4.33. Also included are amendments to the Children Act contained in the Courts and Legal Services Act 1990 and the NHS and Community Care Act 1990, consequential amendments to other pieces of legislation and amendments to existing Children Act Regulations. In addition there is information which will be of assistance to local authorities relating to the new Legal Aid provisions and the Family Court Committee structure established by the Lord Chancellor's Department.

CHAPTER 2 MANAGEMENT OF PANELS OF GUARDIANS AD LITEM AND REPORTING OFFICERS

INTRODUCTION

2.1. This chapter sets out the Guardians ad Litem and Reporting Officers (Panels) Regulations 1991 (reproduced at Annex A) and discusses key areas dealing with the provision of the guardian ad litem and reporting officer (GALRO) service. The power to make Panel Regulations is provided for in section 41(7) of the Children Act, and their scope is governed by the provisions of section 41(9). The function of the service is to safeguard and promote the interests of the child by providing independent social work investigation and advice to the courts in care, child protection, adoption and related court proceedings. Further details as to the specified proceedings where a GALRO may be appointed are set out in paragraphs 2.62 – 2.64 below, and at Annex B.

2.2. Guardians ad litem and reporting officers are not a new creation of the Children Act. Since 1984 the courts have been required to appoint guardians ad litem from panels established by local authorities in accordance with Regulations made under the Children Act 1975. Under the Children Act 1989, however, the role of the guardian ad litem is enhanced. There is a presumption in favour of appointing a guardian ad litem in a wider range of proceedings in the High Court, County Courts and Magistrates Courts. Guardians ad litem are appointed earlier in the proceedings and are charged with playing a full and active role in advising the court on issues of case management, in addition to the role they always had of representing the interests of the child and advising the courts from a social work perspective. They have a proactive role with regard to the conduct of proceedings including timetabling and offering advice to the courts on the range of orders available. The powers and duties of the guardian ad litem in Family Proceedings other than adoption are set out in Rule 11 of the Family Proceedings Courts (Children Act 1989) Rules 1991 (SI 1395/1991) for the magistrates' courts and in Rule 11 of the Family Proceedings Rules 1991 (SI 1247/1991) for the higher courts. In adoption proceedings the role of the GALRO is set out in the Adoption Court Rules. The role of the Official Solicitor acting as a guardian ad litem in High Court proceedings is discussed at paragraphs 2.72 and 2.73 below.

2.3. The duty to provide the GALRO service continues to rest with the local authority (section 41 and the Panel Regulations). The management of the Panel and the payment of fees and allowances to Panel members are the responsibility of the local authority. The tasks, but not the responsibility, may be delegated to other bodies (for example, voluntary organisations) if the local authority chooses to do so (see paragraphs 2.10 *et seq* below).

2.4. The right of children to separate and independent representation in public law hearings is a central tenet of the Children Act. It is essential that GALROs in reaching their judgements about the welfare of each child should continue to be independent of the local authority or other organisation providing the service. Arrangements for the management of the Panel and the day to day work of the GALRO must take full account of this requirement, within the existing legal framework of ultimate accountability residing with the local authority.

2.5. The Act makes it clear that delay in court proceedings is likely to prejudice the child's welfare and must be avoided. It is therefore of particular importance that the Guardian ad Litem service throughout the country is able to respond promptly and effectively to the court demands for individual GALRO appointments in a range of different types of proceedings. Appropriate procedures to assist this process are discussed at paragraphs 2.62 *et seq* below.

2.6. Attention is drawn to the key documentation which is being published to accompany implementation of the Children Act. The 1984 DHSS *"Guide for Guardians ad Litem in the Juvenile Courts"* (known as the "Blue Book") is replaced by the *"Manual of Practice Guidance for Guardians ad Litem and Reporting Officers"*. A companion volume is being prepared – the *"Manual of Practice Guidance for GALRO Panel Managers"*. Panel Managers and Panel Committee members should be familiar with the contents of these documents.

2.7. References in the Regulations to a local authority in the singular should be taken to refer to several local authorities where this is appropriate. This will include where there are reciprocal or consortia arrangements for the provision of the GALRO service. Although the Regulations do not mention voluntary organisations or other forms of administering body, the position of such arrangements is clarified in this guidance.

2.8. The Guardian ad Litem and Reporting Officers (Panels) Regulations 1991 repeal the Panel Regulations made in 1983 and amended in 1986, with effect from 14 October 1991. However, where GALROs are appointed to cases which commenced before 14 October, these cases proceed in accordance with the transitional arrangements set out in Schedule 14 of the Act, the Children Act 1989 (Commencement and Transitional Provisions) Order 1991 and the Children Act 1989 (Commencement No. 2 – Amendment and Transitional Provisions) Order 1991. Further guidance on transitional arrangements will be found in Volume 1 of the guidance and Regulations. Although the DHSS guide *"Panel Administration"* (the 1988 "Green Book") is withdrawn, much of its advice remains valid, and has already been implemented as the basis for the provision of a GALRO service nationally.

MANAGEMENT ARRANGEMENTS FOR THE GALRO SERVICE

Panels of GALROs

2.9. Local authorities should keep under review arrangements for the provision of the establishment of Panels of GALROs in the context of the Children Act legal requirements, the Panel Regulations, the Court Rules, the new court structure and the underlying philosophy of the Act.

2.10. Regulation 2(1) requires that each local authority shall establish a Panel of persons in respect of their area. The statutory responsibility for the establishment of a Panel of guardians continues to rest with local authorities. This responsibility cannot be discharged by other agencies but the day to day tasks can be delegated. Such delegated tasks are discussed later in this chapter in the context of the role of the Panel Committee and the Panel Manager (see paragraphs 2.17–2.33 below).

2.11. Since 1984, a variety of arrangements have developed to take account of varied local circumstances. These include reciprocal arrangements between, usually, two neighbouring authorities, groups of authorities linked loosely or more formally in consortia, single authority Panels and 'contractual' arrangements with voluntary child care organisations. Local authorities have found it advantageous to group together in urban settings; in county areas geographical factors suggest a preference for reciprocal arrangements. However, local authorities, whether contemplating reciprocal or consortia arrangements, will need to weigh up any economies of scale (administrative systems, information technology, flexibility within a larger pool of GALRO skills etc) alongside external complicating factors, in particular the geographical boundaries of the courts at local and higher levels, which tend not to correspond to those of local authorities.

2.12. Changes to such arrangements which existed prior to implementation of the Act may be contemplated. However, there may well be an advantage in postponing for a short while the setting up of new arrangements until a clear pattern of demand for the GALRO service has begun to emerge. Provided that the Panel arrangements achieve the requirements of the Regulations and this guidance, it remains acceptable for local authorities to continue to meet their statutory requirements in any of the ways described above at paragraphs 2.10 and 2.11.

2.13. Regulation 2(2) sets out that GALROs will be appointed to individual cases from Panels established by the local authority in whose area the court is situated. However, some flexibility is allowed which enables GALROs from Panels established elsewhere to be appointed. Such discretion will allow situations to be addressed where there is an exceptional demand which cannot be met from one Panel's membership. One example might be a complex child sexual abuse ring involving a number of children and simultaneous applications. Another example might be in adoption proceedings where a local authority within the catchment area of the Panel places a child outside the Panel area, and the adoption application is made in that area. In such cases it may also be necessary in dealing with the issue of parental consent for the GALRO to travel to the address of the parent(s), which may be in yet another area.

2.14. Panels in certain parts of the country may have to provide a service on a regular basis for courts dealing with applications about children who originate from outside the Panel area. For example, a regional secure unit may be responsible for a significant number of secure accommodation applications per year at the local court, rather than the court in the child's home area. This may place a disproportionate burden on the local Panel if it is felt to be undesirable that a guardian from the Panel which covers the child's home address should deal with the application.

2.15. Depending on the circumstances of each case, it will be for the Panel Manager initially to consider whether it might be more appropriate for a GALRO from their area to undertake the work or whether a GALRO should be requested from another Panel. In the latter situation the court's agreement should be sought. A re-charging arrangement may need to be established between the respective Panels. To avoid confusion, it is suggested that the level of charge to the Panel requesting a GALRO should be that which operates in the Panel from which the GALRO is requested. Panel Managers in such situations should clarify in advance the precise arrangements to be followed. Because of the need to monitor Panel expenditure, re-charging should be conducted on a Panel to Panel basis which either reimburses the fee-attracting GALRO as appropriate, or is otherwise accounted for in respect of non fee-attracting GALROs.

2.16. Regulation 2(3) requires that each local authority shall ensure that so far as possible the numbers of persons appointed to the Panel in their area is sufficient to provide GALROs for all relevant proceedings. Where the task of providing GALROs is delegated to another organisation (for example, a voluntary organisation), then this requirement should be included in the contractual arrangements between the local authority and that organisation, even though legal responsibility remains that of the local authority. The composition of the Panel is discussed below at paragraphs 2.42–2.48.

Administration of Panels

2.17. The successful operation of the GALRO service will depend on a number of important factors. These include the numbers, quality and commitment of individual GALROs, the experience of the Panel Manager, the effectiveness of the Panel Committee and the general level of inter-agency cooperation and co-ordination, particularly with the courts. The Panel Manager will provide a crucial link between the local authority, the courts and the membership of the Panel. The Panel Manager must ensure that the effective deployment of GALRO resources is supported by a comprehensive administrative and financial monitoring system. Further details about the role and function of the Panel Manager are discussed below.

2.18. Each local authority is required to appoint a Panel Manager (Regulation 7(1)). Where the provision of the service is delegated to another organisation, the Panel Manager may be appointed by that organisation on behalf of the local authority. Where local authorities operate reciprocal or consortia arrangements, this may best be achieved by one local authority acting on behalf of the other(s) and dealing with all the appointment, salary and related issues whilst dispersing the costs amongst the participating authorities. Similar arrangements might be made for dealing with premises and administrative staff. *The Panel Manager must not be involved with the authority's services in respect of children and their families except in respect of the Panel and its functions.* Where the size of the Panel does not warrant the appointment of a full- time Panel Manager, a part-time appointment may be considered. In such circumstances it is nevertheless essential that any other responsibilities carried by the Panel Manager should not be in respect of the local authority's services for children and their families. Regulation 7(1) provides an exception whereby a part-time Panel Manager might also have responsibilities within an inspection unit established under the National Health Service and Community Care Act 1990.

2.19. The Panel Manager is employed by the local authority or on their behalf by another organisation. However, the Regulations require that the post is seen to be at "arms length" from the local authority functions in respect of children. Independence will be easier to achieve where Panels are established in consortia or reciprocal arrangements, or delegated to another organisation. Single authority Panels should take particular care to ensure that the post holder is not involved in other tasks where there could be a conflict of interest, especially if the Panel Manager is part-time. Independence will be further enhanced by other practical arrangements such as a direct telephone line; postal address (perhaps as a PO Box rather than the social services address) and appropriately printed letter paper.

2.20. Similar consideration needs to be given in ensuring an appropriate line manager for the Panel Manager. Again, it will be important to avoid any potential conflict of interest where the local authority is a party in court proceedings. As far as practicable the line manager should be located in the management structure of the social services or the local authority's legal services, but avoiding locations which deal predominantly with the provision of child care services or child care legal advice.

2.21. The responsibilities of the Panel Manager are varied and demanding. In addition to the requirements already discussed, the person appointed must have a clear understanding of the duties to be undertaken by GALROs, as set out in the Rules of Court, and the importance of the role overall for the child, the family and the courts. The Panel Manager must be able to deal confidently with the Panel Committee, the GALROs in Panel membership, senior staff in local authorities and, as appropriate, with the voluntary or other organisation providing the service. The Panel Manager is one of those persons listed by the Lord Chancellor's Department whose attendance is expected at the Family Court Business Committee, chaired by the designated Care Centre Judge at the Care Centre covered by the local authority. The Panel Manager will need to have sufficient administrative and clerical assistance in order to service a proper information system and related functions, including the monitoring and processing of financial claims. The Panel Manager, with the help of the Panel Committee, will also need to submit a draft budget to the local authority for the future financial year. This will need to be undertaken at the appropriate stage in the annual local authority financial planning cycle. The Panel Manager will also need to make arrangements for induction and such other training as is appropriate for GALROs (see paragraph 2.86 below). It is expected that in most areas local authorities will wish to ensure that persons appointed as Panel Managers have management, administrative and leadership skills as discussed above. Qualifications and experience in social work, if not an absolute requirement, will be of particular value in a Panel Manager.

2.22. Panel Managers should avoid offering professional consultation or supervision to GALROs in respect of individual cases. This will help to ensure that the individual GALRO is responsible for the judgements necessary as to what is in the interests of the child's welfare in a particular case. However, on broader issues, GALROs may properly wish to use the Panel Manager for consultation, and Panel Managers should be able to provide information directly or sources of information about, for example, procedures, specialist resources or legal issues. Panel Managers should encourage GALROs to provide opportunities amongst themselves for consultation and advice in respect of individual cases. Although Panel Managers are not directly involved in individual cases, they are responsible for setting parameters concerning the overall quality of the service being delivered.

2.23. In summary, the responsibilities of the Panel Manager on behalf of the local authority or other organisation should include:

(a) ensuring an adequate supply of GALROs to the courts at all times and promoting the professional quality of the service;
(b) making arrangements for appropriate training and professional support for GALROs;
(c) arranging for administrative support to Panel members in their tasks;
(d) making appropriate arrangements for the approval and payment of expenses, fees and allowances;
(e) arranging reviews in respect of individual Panel members;
(f) establishing and maintaining an effective management information system;
(g) preparing and managing the Panel budget;
(h) receiving complaints about the service and, where necessary, activating agreed procedures in respect of complaints against GALROs in accordance with the Regulations;
(i) activating the agreed procedures in respect of the termination and non-renewal of Panel membership;
(j) servicing the Panel Committee;
(k) attending the Family Court Business Committee;
(l) preparing the Annual Report on the Panel's activities;
(m) establishing appropriate written procedures for the above;

These issues are discussed at greater length below. The Panel Manager will need to report progress to the Panel Committee on how these responsibilities are being carried out, and whether particular areas need addressing and prioritising. The Panel Committee should be able to provide the Panel Manager with support and direction on policy and procedural matters.

Panel Committee

2.24. Regulation 8 requires the local authority to establish a Panel Committee. The functions of the Committee are derived from the responsibility of the local authority set out in Regulation 8. They are, in broad terms, to assist with liaison between the local authority in their administration of the Panel and the courts in the local authority's area, and to advise them on specific matters (see below).

2.25. A single committee may be set up to serve a consortia of local authorities, local authorities which have set up reciprocal arrangements or a voluntary organisation running a Panel. The terms of reference of the Panel Committee will need to be agreed in writing by the local authority and the Panel Committee, setting out the "contracted" tasks being delegated to the Panel Committee by the local authority. The Regulations give a *minimum* list of tasks that should be included in the terms of reference of the Panel Committee:

"(a) the standards of practice of guardians ad litem and reporting officers in relevant proceedings in their area;

(b) the appointment and reappointment of guardians ad litem and reporting officers to the panel, termination of their appointment and review of their work;

(c) the training of guardians ad litem and reporting officers; and

(d) matters arising from complaints concerning guardians ad litem and reporting officers and the.administration of the panel (but not the investigation of particular complaints)."

Other tasks relating to the Panel Manager's responsibility as set out above at paragraph 2.23 might appropriately be included in the terms of reference.

2.26. The Panel Committee is a vital element in the organisation for the GALRO service. The effectiveness of the Panel Committee will mainly depend on its membership and this should be appointed (by the local authority) in a way which best achieves an appropriate balance within the requirements and discretion of Regulations 3(b) and 8, Schedule 2 and the guidance set out below.

2.27. The Panel Committee has to be established by a local authority under Regulation 3(b). Membership of the Committee is set out in Schedule 2. The membership of the Panel Committee will be drawn from four categories, as defined in Schedule 2 (a)-(d):

"(a) a representative of the local authority;

(b) a justices' clerk of a magistrates' court in the local authority's area;

(c) a person who has relevant experience of child care who is neither an officer nor a member of a local authority;

(d) a representative of the panel established under regulation 2(1) of these Regulations."

The overall size of the Panel Committee is not prescribed by the Regulations. Where Panel Committees already exist, a review of membership should be undertaken to ensure that the requirements of the Regulations are being met. Where local authorities set up Panel Committees where none hitherto have existed, consideration will have to be given to their overall size in relation to the total number of GALROs likely to be in membership. Additional flexibility in membership may also be achieved by co-option and this may be particularly useful where a specialist topic may be under consideration.

2.28. Schedule 2 requires that there be a representative on the Panel Committee of the local authority concerned with the Panel. This may be an officer or a member, and this needs to be determined locally. Local authorities may consider that the Panel's remit suggests attendance at officer level. In the case of consortia or reciprocal arrangements local authorities may share representatives if they so choose.

2.29. Also required is a Justices' Clerk of a magistrates' court. This should be the Clerk to the Justices. Representation from the family proceedings courts is appropriate because of the very high proportion of proceedings where a guardian will be appointed which will be begun and concluded at this level of court.

2.30. The Panel Committee must also include at least one person who has relevant experience of child care and who is neither a local authority officer nor a member of the local authority establishing the Committee. Where the service is being operated on behalf of the local authority by a voluntary organisation, the person appointed under this provision should not be an employee of that organisation or a member of its committee. It may be helpful to include under this category persons with an interest in child care policy and practice, perhaps from a local university department or college offering social work training. The contribution of the Probation service to the Panel might also valuably be reflected on the Panel Committee.

2.31. The fourth category of persons required by Schedule 2 for the Panel Committee is at least one representative of the GALRO membership of that Panel.

2.32. The Panel Committee is also required by Schedule 2 to be chaired by a person who is not a representative of the local authority. This requirement should be borne in mind in considering the overall membership of the Panel and will contribute to the independence of the service, as will a further requirement of the Schedule which states that the membership of the Panel Committee shall not consist of a majority of representatives of the local authority. The Schedule sets out that appointment to the Panel Committee shall be for such period not exceeding three years at any one time as the local authority shall specify in making the appointment. Consideration should be given to the establishment of a procedure which allows for the membership of the Panel Committee to be reviewed at regular intervals and to ensure that the appointment of new members and/or reappointment of existing ones is appropriately dealt with in the course of Panel Committee business.

2.33. The cost of administering the Panel Committee needs to be identified and incorporated into the overall Panel budget. Arrangements for the payment of reasonable expenses incurred by Panel Committee members will have to be agreed. The frequency of Panel Committee meetings will need to be determined locally and will be influenced by the nature of business and the timescales within which discussion ought to be concluded.

Expenses, Fees and Allowances of GALROs

2.34. The local authority is responsible for the reasonable expenses incurred by members of the Panel and the payment of fees and allowances (Regulation 9(1)). However, under Regulation 9(2) expenses, fees and allowances are not payable by the local authority in respect of a member of the Panel who is employed under a contract of service by a local authority or a probation committee for 30 hours or more per week. For persons in these two categories, the payment of their expenses (for example, travelling expenses) is borne directly by the local authority or probation committee rather than through the Panel budget.

2.35. The rates of payment for GALROs are a matter to be determined by local authorities, and are not set nationally. Whatever the scale agreed, it is necessary to differentiate between the rates for different types of GALRO activities, such as travelling, court attendance and report writing. Panel Managers, as noted above, are responsible for ensuring that there is a comprehensive analysis of fees and expenses claimed by individual GALROs. This in turn allows for ongoing monitoring of expenditure against a planned budget. If it appears to the Panel Manager that anticipated expenditure in relation to fees and expenditure is likely to exceed the budget within any given financial year, the situation must be reported at the earliest opportunity with full supporting details to the local authority responsible for establishing the Panel (or to the voluntary organisation responsible for providing the service on behalf of a local authority). The local authority will then be in a position to review the funding arrangements in the context of its statutory responsibility for the GALRO service.

2.36. Panel Committees and Panel Managers will wish to ensure that expenses, fees and allowances claimed by GALROs are proper and reasonable. Clear procedures should be agreed with the Panel membership, the Panel Committee and the local authority (or voluntary organisation on their behalf) to facilitate the prompt payment of expenses, fees and allowances. In most cases the details provided on the claim form will satisfy the general criteria as to whether the expenses were reasonable and necessary for the proper performance of the Panel member' s duties under the legislation, including the time actually and reasonably spent on the case by the Panel member. Where the guardian anticipates that unusual or substantial expenses may be necessary, it would be good practice to alert the Panel Manager to the relevant facts. This may arise because, for example, there are a number of children for whom the guardian is acting, perhaps placed at some distance in various locations and with different parental figures to be interviewed. In adoption matters, it may be that the issue of parental consent needs careful exploration by interview but that the relevant parent is currently resident outside the UK. Where the GALRO needs to make use of medical and other services which are part of the National Health Service, the local authority should arrange for these to be obtained where possible under existing collaborative arrangements. A GALRO who seeks separate legal representation is not eligible for legal aid (SI 1991/2036, Annex K) and the local authority is liable to meet the costs.

2.37. GALROs need to judge the extent of enquiries necessary in each individual case to which they are appointed. If there is uncertainty as to whether in a particular case the work proposed by the GALRO is appropriate and necessary, then the proper channel for this to be clarified is likely to be through the directions hearing under the provisions of the Rules of Court (Rules 14 and 11(4)(f)) or equivalent advice and direction from the court dealing with the adoption proceedings.

2.38. Where a GALRO's pattern of claims or an individual claim appears markedly different to those submitted by other GALROs in comparable cases, the Panel Manager will need to discuss the issues with the individual concerned. This proper function of the Panel Manager in respect of accounting for the Panel budget requires sensitive handling to avoid any inference that the independent judgement of a guardian in a particular case is being undermined. If a dispute arises as to the professional aspects of a GALRO's performance, it may need to be resolved by the Panel Committee.

APPOINTMENT OF PANEL MEMBERS

Number of guardians

2.39. The pattern of demand for guardians will be subject to variation and it is apparent that many factors will affect the overall numbers of applications and hence the number of appointments of GALROs. Some of these factors will tend to reduce and others will increase the numbers of appointments required. The Children Act intends that, where possible, arrangements for children should be reached without recourse to court but where an order is necessary for the child's welfare, it is the court's duty to have the child's welfare as the paramount consideration.

2.40. Panels which have monitored applications carefully prior to the implementation of the Act may be in a better position to anticipate the likely demand for guardians. However, post-implementation, thorough monitoring of trends will also be an important aid for Panel Managers in ensuring that an adequate supply of GALROs is available and that on appointment they can commence their work promptly.

2.41. A further factor to be taken into account in calculating the numbers of GALROs who should be in membership of the Panel will be whether they are part time or full time. This is discussed below in respect of Regulation 4 and the role of the Panel Committee. Panel Committees, Managers and guardians will all wish to avoid the extremes of there either being too few GALROs to meet the overall court demands or the converse, where there is insufficient work to share amongst the GALRO membership if retained at a particular size and make up.

Panel Membership

2.42. The membership of the Panel should reflect the need for a flexible approach to appointment in individual cases. Where possible, the particular characteristics of the child and the identities of the parties to the proceedings will determine the choice of GALRO. The Rules of Court and this guidance set out principles which establish the independence of the GALRO in court proceedings and associated standards of good practice.

2.43. The Panel membership should, where possible, comprise individuals drawn from the following categories:

— self-employed social workers (full-time or part-time);
— employees of a local authority (full-time or part-time);
— employees of a voluntary organisation (full-time or part-time).
— probation officers;

Those persons who are employed part-time as probation officers may, in the remainder of their time, act as Panel members in respect of care and adoption proceedings, whereas if they are panel members as serving probation officers their role is restricted to adoption proceedings.

2.44. The Rules of Court set out four categories of persons who, although they may be in membership of the Panel, must not be appointed for specified proceedings (as set out in section 41(6) and Court Rule 2(2)) in particular cases. Rule 10(7) (see Annex B) states that, subject to certain exceptions – discussed below in paragraph 2.45 – those excluded from appointment to certain cases are Panel members who are:

— a member, officer or servant of a local authority where that local authority is a party to the proceedings (unless employed solely as a Panel member);
— a member, officer or servant of the NSPCC where that organisation is bringing proceedings under section 31 and other sections of the Act;
— a serving probation officer;
— a member, officer or servant of a local authority or voluntary organisation involved or who have been involved, with that child (see paragraph 2.45 below).

2.45. Whether Panel members are employed solely by local authorities as Panel members full-time or part-time, or are employed by voluntary organisations, the intention of Court Rule 10(7)(b) is to ensure that a guardian is not appointed to a case if formerly that person *"has been directly concerned in that capacity in arrangements relating to the care, accommodation or welfare of the child during the five years prior to the commencement of the proceedings"*. As stated above, a serving probation officer who is employed part-time may act in remaining time as a guardian in specified proceedings, provided that as a probation officer he has not *"been concerned with the child or his family"* (Rule 10(7)(c)).

2.46. Situations may arise where, although the GALRO is currently a self-employed social worker in Panel membership, at an earlier date that person was employed by the local authority or voluntary organisation and in that capacity was directly involved with the care of the child within five years of the present proceedings. It may be that the GALRO's prior involvement with the family dates back further than five years. A GALRO may not realise their previous involvement in a non-GALRO role with the family (if names and addresses have changed) until they meet the family. In all these kinds of situations the GALRO must avoid any suggestion of bias because of previous knowledge of the child derived from former work in a non-GALRO capacity. Furthermore, indirect knowledge of a child may be obtained from professional or personal links with a person who is, or who has been, closely involved with a child or family. For example, the GALRO's spouse may be employed by the local authority that is a party to the proceedings and may have been concerned with the child or family. It is strongly recommended in this guidance that in any of these kinds of situations, the GALRO advises the court of the reason why an alternative GALRO appointment should be made.

2.47. However, examples given above of personal knowledge of the child which might affect the GALRO's ability to reach an independent judgement about the child's welfare need to be distinguished from other circumstances, such as the GALRO's previous employment, where prior knowledge of the particular child is not in question. That a GALRO may have previously been employed by the local authority or voluntary organisation involved in the court proceedings should not place at risk the GALRO's ability to reach an independent conclusion about the child's welfare.

2.48. Where Panels have consortia or reciprocal arrangements the possibility of a GALRO employed by a local authority having knowledge of a particular case will be reduced but not removed. It will also be easier for alternative GALROs to be found. Single authority Panels will need to ensure that flexibility to provide suitable GALROs is not restricted by drawing a large proportion of their membership from the category of employee of the local authority, particularly if those persons formerly were employed as social workers with a child care remit in that local authority.

Appointment Process

2.49. Appointments of GALROs to the Panel are the formal responsibility of the local authority in whose area the Panel is established (Regulation 4(1)). The practical steps in the appointment process may be undertaken by the Panel Committee. The need for a broad membership offering flexibility has already been discussed in the preceding paragraphs.

2.50. In deciding how persons might be recruited, the views of the Panel Committee would be appropriate. In considering the overall membership of the Panel, attention is drawn to the requirement under Regulation 4(6) that the local authority should have regard to the number of children in their area who may become the subject of specified proceedings (ie proceedings defined at section 41(6) and Court Rule 2(2)) and the different racial groups to which they belong. The intention here is to allow, as far as practicable, flexibility in matching the type of proceedings and needs of the child to the characteristics and skills of the guardian. Whilst in general terms it should be possible for a guardian to undertake duties in respect of the full range of potential cases, there will be certain situations where it is particularly important that the guardian selected be of the same sex, race, language, culture or religion of the child and the family. In cases involving children with disabilities a guardian may have to call on additional specialist assistance. Similarly, where it is not possible to appoint a guardian who speaks the same language as the child or the child's family, an interpreter will be necessary.

2.51. It is expected that most GALROs will be qualified in social work and also have several years of relevant expertise working with children. They will need an aptitude for the demands and discipline for the type of work. Regulation 4(2) requires that the local authority determines the eligibility criteria for GALROs. Exceptionally, they may conclude that an applicant, although not possessing a formal qualification in social work, does have relevant experience and qualifications which makes appointment or reappointment appropriate. It should be remembered that experience of social work with children and families is not in itself sufficient for Panel membership. The role of the GALRO also requires knowledge of and skills in planning for children in care and adoption work. Regulation 4(3) requires that the procedures for appointment to the Panel include that the prospective Panel member be interviewed, that the Panel Committee be consulted and that at least two written references are obtained. The choice of referees is potentially broad. Panel Committees may consider that it would be appropriate for one of these to be from a recent or the most recent employer. A check should also be made with the Department of Health's Consultancy Service and prospective members informed that this will be done. Consultation with the Panel Committee in respect of possible new appointees should be distinguished from the involvement of the Panel Committee in the interview process discussed below. Consultation with the Panel Committee is likely to be most effective if confined to broader policy issues. For example, the Panel Committee may have a policy objective of achieving an appropriate balance of GALROs by gender, race and category (as described above at paragraph 2.50).

2.52. All applicants accepted as potentially appropriate for appointment should be interviewed. The interviewing Panel should comprise, at least, one representative of the Panel Committee, the Panel Manager and a person who is independent of the local authority. This person should have knowledge of the court- related issues and the child care situations with which a GALRO would typically expect to be involved. The conditions, expectations and requirements of the appointment should be fully discussed at interview. Expectations about the availability of and attendance at induction and further training should be clarified.

2.53. A clear job description based on the Rules of Court and details of complaints, reappointment, termination, and review procedures should be made available together with a general statement setting out the Panel's organisation. Regulation 4(4) requires that the appointment as a GALRO should be for such period not exceeding three years at any one time. Appointments should be confirmed in writing by the local authority. Letters of appointment should be approved by the local authority's legal advisors. Letters should contain such conditions, expectations and requirements of service as are discussed below. The letter of appointment should be clear that appointment is not a contract of employment. However, where local authorities employ a guardian solely as a member of a Panel, the written arrangements will be different and these will need to be reflected in the letter of appointment. Similar considerations arise in relation to Panel members from the probation service.

2.54. Letters of appointment should also contain a requirement that where the appointment of a guardian ad litem is not renewed or is terminated, the guardian ad litem must return to the Panel Manager any letter of appointment, authorised photograph of identity and records relating to work undertaken in individual cases. Whilst working as a GALRO, the individual guardian ad litem must, of course, have scrupulous regard to the issues of confidentiality. Information gained in the course of performing their functions remains confidential after the GALRO ceases to be a member of the Panel. Letters of appointment should therefore also make clear that any information obtained in the course of GALRO duties with regard to an individual child and her family cannot be used were that GALRO to cease to be a member of the Panel and undertake work in some other capacity such as, for example, a social work consultant.

2.55. Exceptionally, circumstances may arise where a number of guardians ad litem have to be appointed simultaneously in related proceedings (see paragraph 2.13 above). If the Panel has insufficient guardians to cope with the sudden demand, it will be appropriate for the Panel Manager to seek the co-operation of neighbouring Panels. Such temporary arrangements will require written confirmation dealing with inter-Panel charging (if necessary).

Reappointment

2.56. Regulation 4(4) allows a GALRO's appointment to be renewed. There is no automatic entitlement that the GALRO should be reappointed, although this may frequently happen. The procedure for reappointment will need to include key elements from Regulation 4 – particularly Regulation 4(3) (a), that the person be interviewed, and Regulation 4(3)(b), that the Panel Committee be consulted. If the GALRO is not reappointed then, should they so wish, they may make a complaint under Regulation 6 (see paragraphs 2.89–2.95 below).

Termination of Appointment

2.57. The appointment of a member of the Panel may be terminated by the local authority at any time (Regulation 5(1)). The grounds for termination are:

(i) that the guardian is unable to carry out the functions of a GALRO; or

(ii) that the guardian is unfit to carry out functions of a GALRO;

The ground of unfitness will principally concern issues of professional competence. The ground at (i) above may be triggered by the GALRO's own request due for example, to a change in domestic, employment or residence circumstances.

2.58. Termination of a person's membership of the Panel is a serious step which needs to be subject to formal procedures. The Regulations therefore place on the local authority a number of requirements which must be met before terminating a person's membership. In the following paragraphs, the guidance in respect of Panels operated by voluntary organisations or other bodies on behalf of a local authority applies to them rather than the local authority. The local authority will need to ensure that the voluntary organisation or other body follows these procedures:

— The local authority must notify the GALRO in writing of the reasons why it is proposed that membership of the Panel should be terminated (Regulation 5(2)(a));

— The GALRO must be given an opportunity to make representations to the local authority (Regulation 5(2)(b)). This should normally be done within 21 days of the receipt of the notification;

— Where the local authority having considered such representations, still propose to terminate that person's membership, they shall refer the matter to a complaint's board established by the authority (Regulations 1(2) and 3(a)).

— The complaints board should consist of three persons:

"*(a) one of whom shall be a person who is neither an officer nor a member of a local authority;*

(b) another of whom shall be a person who is involved in the functions in respect of services for children and their families of a local authority which has not established the panel;

(c) another of whom shall be a justices' clerk of a magistrates' court in the local authority's area" (Schedule 1)

— The complaints board must make a recommendation to the local authority on the question of termination after taking into account any representations of the person whose membership the local authority propose to terminate (Regulation 5(4));

— Having considered the recommendation of the complaints board, the local authority must give notice to the member in writing of their decision whether or not to terminate membership, together with their reasons for the decision (Regulation 5(5)).

Other issues concerning complaints are dealt with below at paragraph 2.89 *et seq.*

2.59. There may be exceptional circumstances (such as the arrest of the GALRO in respect of Schedule 1 offences) where the immediate suspension of membership is required. Immediate suspension should only be invoked where the seriousness of the allegations pose an obvious risk to any child with whom the GALRO is currently working. Suspension does not imply guilt but does necessitate that the GALRO should not undertake duties until the matter has been clarified. In such circumstances the Panel Manager, with the advice of the Panel Committee, should contact the local authority forthwith. Where the suspended GALRO is in membership of more than one Panel, the Panel Manager should inform all the relevant Panels of the suspension. If the GALRO has current duties in respect of one or more cases, the Panel Manager should liaise with the court(s) who appointed the GALRO to the case(s). The Court Rules allow for the appointment of a guardian in a particular case to be terminated by the court and a new guardian to be appointed. This is a matter for the court and separate from issues of termination of membership.

2.60. It is important that procedures dealing with matters of termination and suspension should be completed within reasonable timescales. Panel Committees may wish to discuss such procedures with the local authorities so that all concerned are aware of the proposed time scales. Although time scales will not be legally binding, they will give an indication of appropriate professional practice. Where termination, suspension or non-renewal of a GALRO appointment occurs in respect of a person who is an employee of the local authority or probation service (or voluntary organisation) it will also be necessary to give the employer the relevant information concerning the matter.

Record of Appointment of Members

2.61. There is a requirement at Regulation 4(5) that each local authority shall maintain a record of those persons whom they have appointed to be members of the Panel established in respect of their area. This record serves a number of purposes, including providing an accessible source of information about the dates of appointment, reappointment, review and termination of Panel membership of GALROs; the gender and racial balance achieved by the Panel; the category of GALRO (probation, local authority, fee attracting – see above) and other information valuable for management purposes. These details may therefore need to be reported upon to the Panel Committee at regular intervals. Some of this information will also be relevant to the annual report which is discussed later in the guidance.

CASE ALLOCATION

2.62. The range of proceedings where guardians may be appointed is extended under the Children Act from former legislation. Section 41(6)(a) to (h) sets out the types of proceedings. These are:

- an application for a care order or supervision order (section 31); where the court has directed the local authority to undertake an investigation of the child's circumstances and has made, or is considering whether to make, an interim care order (sections 37(1) and 38(1)(a));
- an application for the discharge of a care order or the variation or discharge of a supervision order (section 39);
- an application to substitute a supervision order for a care order (section 39(4));
- in which the court is considering whether to make a residence order with respect to a child who is the subject of a care order (section 8);
- with respect to contact between a child who is the subject of a care order and any other person (section 34);
- under Part V, applications for a child assessment order (section 43); an emergency protection order (section 44); the extension of an emergency protection order (section 45);the variation and discharge of a child assessment order and emergency protection order (section 45);
- appeals arising from the making, or the refusal to make a care order, supervision order, contact order or residence order (with respect to a child who is the subject of a care order);

— appeals arising from the variation or discharge (or refusal of an application to vary or discharge) the orders listed in the above paragraph;

— appeals arising from the refusal to substitute a supervision order for a care order;

— appeals arising from the making or refusal to make an order under Part V.

2.63. Under the provisions of section 41(6)(i) four additional categories of cases are named as "specified proceedings" in Rule (2) of the Family Proceedings Rules and the Family Proceedings Courts (Children Act 1989) Rules. These are:

— proceedings under section 25 for a secure accommodation order;

— applications under section 33(7) for the leave of court to the proposed change of surname for a child who is the subject of a care order or the proposed removal of such a child from the United Kingdom;

— applications under paragraph 19(1) of Schedule 2 for the arranging or assistance in arranging for a child in care of the local authority to live outside England and Wales;

— applications under paragraph 6(3) of Schedule 3 for the extension, or further extension of a supervision order originally made under section 31.

— Rules of Court also specify appeals arising from these proceedings.

2.64. Guardians ad litem and reporting officers will continue to be required in adoption proceedings as set out in the rules made under section 65 of the Adoption Act 1976 (amended to take into account the Children Act.)

2.65. Delays in appointing GALROs undermine one of the central principles of the Children Act, regarding the avoidance of delay. The Panel Manager has to deploy the resources of the Panel as effectively as possible and have regard to the overall costs and finite budget within which the service operates. The courts need to have GALROs available to be appointed and to commence work promptly. Since 1985 different appointment procedures have evolved throughout the country. This has meant in some areas that the courts are provided with Panel lists of GALROs and court staff telephone around to find a GALRO available to be appointed. In other areas the selection of a GALRO is undertaken on behalf of the court by the Panel Manager and the court is advised which GALRO to appoint.

2.66. Under the Children Act responsibility for deciding that a GALRO is needed and the sending out of the notice of appointment (form CHA 30 in the Rules of Court in respect of guardians ad litem) remains a function of the court. Existing arrangements between the court and the Panel Manager should be reviewed. It is recommended that, where possible, and with the court's agreement, the initial selection of a GALRO for the court should be undertaken by the Panel Manager. This will allow the most effective deployment of the Panel resources and will facilitate where practicable improved matching between the needs of an individual case (as it appears at the application stage) and the skills or other attributes of particular GALROs. At the same time the Panel Manager will have an overview of the distribution of work across the Panel and the availability of individual GALROs in terms of their current workload and other commitments, such as annual leave or training.

2.67. Where exceptionally a Panel serves a large number of courts, the preferred approach outlined above may not be feasible. Nevertheless, the arrangements for allocating work should be kept under review and may usefully be discussed at the Family Court Business Committee.

2.68. Where the Official Solicitor is appointed he will allocate the case to a member of his staff (see paragraphs 2.72–2.73 below).

Arrangements for emergency protection and other orders

2.69. It will be necessary to have in place arrangements to ensure the immediate appointment of a guardian where an emergency protection order has been applied for. Such hearings may be *inter partes* applications. *Ex parte* applications for emergency protection orders have to follow the procedures set out in the Court Rules, which include the requirement that leave of the Clerk be obtained. Applications may be in usual court hours or out of court hours. In exceptional circumstances, telephone applications may be allowed. The court's expectations of the guardian ad litem service where the initial application is being dealt with are likely to be limited. Panel Managers should make arrangements for exceptional appointments with the Clerks at the Family Proceedings Courts in their areas. On appointment, the guardian ad litem will be required to undertake whatever duties are practicable in the time available and as set out in the Court Rules. Emergency protection orders may be discharged after 72 hours. Not all cases will come to a hearing after 72 hours but, for those that do, it will again be necessary for Panel Managers and the Clerks to clarify expectations for this stage in the proceedings.

2.70. Although Clerks are likely to operate a duty system whereby they can be contacted out of hours for such *ex parte* applications, it is not considered necessary that a large number of guardians in any one area should similarly be on standby, but there will need to be a procedure whereby a guardian can be contacted at very short notice. Local authorities will need to estimate the likely numbers of such proceedings and how the availability of a guardian ad litem can be assured in the most practical and cost-effective manner. Local discussion between the Panel Manager and the Clerks will also be fruitful in reaching agreement as to the expectations when a GALRO appointed at short notice exceptionally might not continue work with that particular case if further proceedings are then initiated.

2.71. Consideration should also be given to the need to appoint a guardian ad litem quickly in cases other than emergency protection orders. For example, there may be applications under section 31 of the Act where the local authority is requesting an interim order at the first hearing. This would necessitate the guardian ad litem being available promptly to make a preliminary investigation within a few days of appointment in time for the first hearing.

The Official Solicitor

2.72. Under directions pursuant to the provisions of section 41(8), the role of the Official Solicitor includes the duty to act as guardian ad litem in certain High Court proceedings. The proceedings where the Official Solicitor will be appointed are those which commence and are completed in the High Court or which are allocated to the High Court from a lower court and, in either case, no guardian ad litem has been appointed and there are exceptional circumstances which call for Official Solicitor involvement rather than a Panel guardian. When acting as a guardian ad litem, the Official Solicitor's duties will be those required of all guardians ad litem as set out in Rule 11 of the Rules of Court. The Official Solicitor will not be in membership of any Panel of guardians ad litem.

2.73. The Official Solicitor and his staff have great expertise in regard to High Court procedures and child care cases where wider issues of public policy and complexity are present. The frequent use of experts such as paediatricians and child psychiatrists in High Court proceedings has also afforded the Official Solicitor an opportunity to have access to such specialists nationwide and their knowledge will be of value to guardians ad litem. Panel Managers should establish liaison links between their Panel and the Official Solicitor so that Panel guardians ad litem may have access to such specialists if the need arises in a particular case.

The functions of the GALRO

2.74. The powers and duties of the guardian ad litem on appointment are set out in the Rules of Court (Rule 11 – see Annex B). In adoption matters the roles of the guardian ad litem are set out in the Adoption Court Rules. The purpose of having effective management arrangements for the GALRO service is to ensure that GALROs are able to operate as skilled and confident professionals and are supported in carrying out their powers and duties. Efficient mechanisms for case allocation are another key element in achieving overall a sensible deployment of GALRO resources. Similarly, the issues dealt with in the following section on monitoring, review and training are all aimed at enhancing the quality of service for children and families in court proceedings.

Access to Records

2.75. The right of the guardian ad litem to have access to local authority records (and authorised persons) is set out in the Children Act at section 42 (as amended by the Courts and Legal Services Act 1990). Where the guardian ad litem proposes that records prepared in contemplation of proceedings shall be adduced in court, the procedure is governed by rule 18 of the Court Rules. The right of access does not extend to records held by health authorities, but health records included in the local authority records form part of that local authority's records. Should guardians experience difficulties in obtaining a satisfactory level of co-operation, it may be necessary for a more formal approach to be made by the Panel Manager or the local authority. The Children Act 1989 does not alter the position in respect of adoption applications and GALROs in such proceedings continue to have right of access to adoption agency records.

Confidentiality and Storage of Records

2.76. Local authorities will need to review arrangements whereby GALROs are provided with typing services for correspondence and court reports or where such GALROs not employed by the local authority make independent arrangements for such typing to be undertaken. The confidential and sensitive nature of GALRO work requires that, whatever the arrangements, there should be the clearest written undertaking to preserve confidentiality. The need for records to be returned to safe storage on a long-term basis relates to further possible court cases including, for example, claims for compensation or proceedings under the European Convention on Human Rights. Further guidance will be issued on the circumstances and time limits for storage but until then such records should not be destroyed. Arrangements should also cover the erasing of information in the form of correspondence and reports held on word processors. Records need to be securely stored, and the local authority and Panel Manager should ensure adequate arrangements are made following discussion with the courts. The long-term storage of records at the GALRO's home address is strongly discouraged and practical arrangements and expectations about short-term storage arrangements should be discussed between the GALRO, the Panel Manager and the Panel Committee. These must include safeguards against theft and unauthorised access.

MONITORING, REVIEW, TRAINING AND COMPLAINTS

Monitoring

2.77. An essential mechanism for effective monitoring will be the existence of a comprehensive information system, as required by Regulation 7(2).

2.78. The use of information technology packages is highly desirable. The purpose of such a system is to ensure effective day to day monitoring and the capacity for detailed analysis of information at regular intervals. The Panel Committee, the courts and the local authority will wish to know the overall demand for GALROs and which levels of courts are requiring the GALRO service. The Panel Manager will also need to be in a position to inform guardians and other relevant persons about the overall performance of the service, including whether guardians have commenced work promptly and the length of time different types of proceeding have taken. A further requirement will be for financial monitoring of the overall budget, preparation of future budgets and the prompt servicing of claims for expenses and fees. These and related issues are brought together in Regulation 7(2)(a)–(g), as a *minimum* list of the information to be routinely collected. Managers will wish to discuss with their Panels whether other data should be routinely collected, analysed and reported on.

2.79. Regulation 7(2) states that:

> *"Each local authority shall ensure that records are kept in relation to the operation of the panel which shall include–*
>
> *(a) the name of the child in respect of whom a guardian ad litem or reporting officer is selected from the panel;*
>
> *(b) a description of the relevant proceedings in respect of which the appointment is made;*
>
> *(c) the name and level of the court (whether High Court, county court or family proceedings court);*
>
> *(d) the name of any person selected from the panel and whether he has been appointed in specified proceedings or in proceedings under the Adoption Act 1976 as a guardian ad litem, or under the Adoption Act 1976 as a reporting officer;*
>
> *(e) the date of each appointment, the date on which work started in respect of that appointment and the date on which it finished;*
>
> *(f) details of fees, expenses and allowances in each case in which there has been such an appointment;*
>
> *(g) the result of the proceedings in each case in which there has been such an appointment."*

2.80. Information provided by effective monitoring processes will contribute to the regular dialogue between Panel Managers and GALROs regarding the professional expectations of the service and how these might be translated into qualitative and quantitative statements. Panel Managers will need to be proactive in addressing these issues, which form core elements for the professionally managed GALRO service. The Panel Committee and GALRO members will all be concerned to ensure that professional standards for the service are set as high as can be realistically achieved and fully reflect the demands of the new legislative framework and philosophy.

2.81. Additional information, such as the age, race, culture religion and language of the child and family, and family characteristics will be of value. It will be useful to have some record of the guardian's recommendation so that this can be compared with the orders made by the court. Where a court at a Directions Hearing requests a GALRO to carry out specific duties, these should be recorded and kept for analysis. Overall monitoring will also provide valuable information to be included in the annual report, discussed at paragraph 2.85 below.

Review

2.82. Regulation 10(1) states:

> *"For the purposes of monitoring the work of guardians ad litem and reporting officers each local authority which has established a panel in respect of their area shall–*
>
> *(a) obtain the views of the panel committee on the work of each member of the panel who has been appointed a guardian ad litem or reporting officer, and*

(b) *review the work of each member of the panel at least once during the first year of an appointment to the panel."*

2.83. The requirement that each GALRO's work is reviewed at least once during the first year of an appointment to the Panel means, for example, that where a GALRO is appointed under Regulation 4(4) for a three year period, and is reappointed at the end of the period, the GALRO will have at least one review in year one and a second in year four. Panel Committees already operating review systems will wish to review their current arrangements in the light of the Regulations. For Panels newly establishing a review system, the first task will be to set out the procedure and the details of how the Panel members, the Panel Committee and Panel Manager should best be involved in a fair appraisal system. In this context, Panel Committees should agree how best they can provide views as to the work of each GALRO as required by Regulation 10(1)(a). In many situations this may best be achieved by the involvement of the panel membership in the review discussion with individual GALRO's. A procedure will also be needed to make available copies of the GALRO's reports as part of the review process. Information identifying the name of the child and family should be deleted.

2.84. In accordance with general principles of openness, the results of each Review are required by Regulation 10(2) to be recorded in writing by the local authority. A copy of the results of the Review has to be sent to the member of the Panel to whom they relate.

Annual report

2.85. There should be an annual report provided by each Panel in respect of the year ending 31st March, and this should be published not later than 30th June. The framework for the annual report should be agreed by the Panel Committee. It should include a summary of the activity of the Panel Members (see paragraph 2.79); the breakdown of financial expenditure; membership of the Panel Committee; membership of the Panel (ie type of GALRO and work undertaken by each); training activities; key policy and practice developments (for example, by meetings with the Family Court Business Committee); priorities to be addressed in the period to be covered by the next report. Copies of the Annual Report should be made available to the local authority's Social Services Committee, the Family Court Business Committee and the Department of Health (Branch CS3D, Room 237, Wellington House, 133–155 Waterloo Road, London SE1 8UG), as well as the Panel Committee and the Panel GALRO membership.

Training

2.86. Regulation 11 states that:

"the local authority shall, having regard to the cases in which members of the panel have been or may have been appointed as a guardian ad litem or reporting officer, identify any training need which members of the panel may have and make reasonable provision for such training"

The training of Panel members is important. Panel members appointed are expected to have a proven record of professional competence. However, all newly appointed Panel members should be offered a period of induction training. It may be appropriate for the provision of induction training to be a shared arrangement between several Panels in a region.

2.87. Additional training in respect of more specialist subjects may also be required. Depending on the terms of delegation to the Panel Committee, a training strategy will need to be developed and kept under review. Expectations as to what levels of training should reasonably be funded from the Panel budget and what other sources of funding might be available, will need to be explored.

2.88. In complex and difficult cases GALROs may well need to call on the expertise of specialists. Reference has already been made at paragraphs 2.36 and 2.73 to the need for access to specialist help. Depending on the issues, it may be necessary for such persons to see the child (providing prior leave of court has been granted in accordance with the Court Rules) or it may be sufficient for the GALRO to use the specialist in a consultancy role in order to discuss aspects of the case. Panel Managers will need to know the range of specialists required and, if used in the consultancy role, clarify any requirements for remuneration. The role of the Panel Manager is to make available such information as a guardian may find of assistance. It is not to advise that a particular specialist should be used by a guardian, as this is the responsibility of the GALRO in the exercise of their professional judgement or with the assistance of the court. It may be particularly useful for Panel Managers to share between Panels the sources of such specialist advice. The arrangements for doing this might be discussed at the Family Court Business Committee.

Complaints about the Operation of the GALRO Service

2.89. Reference has been made at paragraph 2.39 et seq to the Complaints Board established by Regulation 3(a) and how GALROs might use the procedure in respect of matters relating to their membership of the Panel. This section of the guidance discusses the complaints procedure in respect of the operation of the Panel Committee, GALRO Panel members and the Panel Manager. There may be a variety of sources of possible complaints. For example, a party to the proceedings or another professional (solicitor, doctor) or agency (the court, the police) may wish to lodge adverse comment in respect of the guardian ad litem's professional work. Courts may feel (notwithstanding discussion at the Family Court Business Committee) that a formal complaint about particular shortcomings of the GALRO service should be directed at the Panel Manager. The local authority responsible for the service may wish formally to complain about the failure of the Panel Manager or Panel Committee to meet an agreed target.

2.90. Regulation 6(1) states that:

> *"For the purpose of monitoring the administration and procedures of the panel and the work of guardians ad litem and reporting officers in relevant proceedings each local authority shall establish a procedure for considering complaints about the operation of the panel in respect of their area, and about any member of that panel including refusal to reappoint a person to be a panel member"*

2.91. Regulation 6(2) requires the local authority to

> *"investigate any such complaint and if they cannot resolve it to the satisfaction of the person making it they shall refer it to the complaints board to make a recommendation to the authority about it in writing."*

As part of the general arrangements and procedures between the local authority responsible for the GALRO service and the Panel Committee, it will be necessary to harmonise the receipt of complaints about the GALRO service and the initial handling by the local authority with the local authority's own complaints procedures. This should avoid inappropriate overlap and potential confusion between complaints being dealt with by the local authority and those being addressed within the Panel's Complaints Board procedures. Depending on the source of the complaint and its nature it may be possible for the matter to be satisfactorily resolved without recourse to the Complaints Board – indeed this is usually the first option to be explored.

2.92. The Complaints Board, as established in accordance with Schedule 1 is not necessarily intended to be of fixed membership. For reasons set out below, fixed membership would not be desirable. For each complaint being dealt with, the principle of independence will need to be addressed. One member of the Board should be a person who is neither an officer nor a member of a local authority. Another member has to have day-to-day local authority experience of local authority services for children and their families, but the person should not be working for the local authority which established the Panel (or, if the complaint is from another local authority, that particular authority). The third member should be a justices' clerk of a magistrates' court in the local authority's area in which relevant proceedings are heard. Since there will be a number of courts able to hear proceedings under the Act within the local authority (i.e, GALRO Panel) catchment area, this again allows flexibility in choice if, for example, the source of complaint is a court. The Panel Committee should establish some basic procedures and consider reciprocal arrangements with neighbouring Panels to enhance objectivity.

2.93. Regulation 6(3) states that:

> *"Any person in respect of whom a complaint is made shall be notified by the local authority in writing of the complaint and they shall give him an opportunity of making representations to them and if the matter is referred to the complaints board shall provide him with an opportunity to make representations to the complaints board."*

Where the Complaints Board becomes involved, then it may usually be helpful for it to set out the arrangements covering the receipt of representations.

2.94. Regulation 6(4) requires that:

> *"The local authority shall only make a decision on a complaint referred to the complaints board having taken into account the recommendation of the complaints board and they shall notify the person who made the complaint and any person in respect of whom the complaint was made in writing of their decision."*

Depending on arrangements agreed between the local authority and the Panel Committee, it may be in many situations preferable for the Panel Committee to make the decision on behalf of the local authority and deal with the notifications required by Regulations 6(3) and 6(4).

2.95. The complaint provision in the Regulations have to take account of the differing structures providing the GALRO service as discussed above at paragraph 2.11. Whilst many complaints may originate from sources external to these structures, some may be internal (for example, a dispute between the Panel Committee and the Panel Manager, or between the Panel Committee and the local authority). Resort to a complaints procedure may well be rendered unnecessary by the establishment of proper, open avenues of communications and opportunities to resolve differences before they reach the status of formal complaints.

CHAPTER 3 EDUCATION SUPERVISION ORDERS

INTRODUCTION

3.1. Under the Children Act 1989, it is no longer possible to seek a care or supervision order on educational grounds alone. The specific grounds in the Children and Young Persons Act 1969, including section 1(2)(e) which allowed for a care order to be sought if the child was not receiving proper education are repealed. The legislation also amends the Education Act 1944 so that courts may no longer direct that care proceedings be taken with regard to a child whose parents have been prosecuted under section 39 of the 1944 Act.

3.2. Section 36 of the Children Act empowers local education authorities to apply to the courts for an education supervision order putting under their supervision a child of compulsory school age who is not being properly educated. The Act and this guidance seek to provide a framework for good professional practice in relation to the education supervision order which includes cooperation between local education authorities, schools and parents. The intention is to ensure that a child who is subject to the order receives efficient full-time education suited to his or her age, ability, aptitude and any special educational needs, and that sufficient support, advice and guidance are provided to the parents and the child.

Scope of legislation

3.3. Section 36 (3) of the Act provides for an education supervision order to be made only if the court is satisfied that a child of compulsory school age is not being properly educated, but an order may not be made with respect to a child already in care of the local authority (section 36 (6)). The local authority's general responsibility to ensure that children of compulsory school age receive efficient full-time education suitable to age, ability, aptitude and any special educational needs extends to children in care. Paragraph 12 of Schedule 3 provides that directions attached to the order apply both to the child and to the parents of the child. The parents are taken to include any person who is not a parent but who has parental responsibility towards the child or a person who has care of the child (paragraph 21 of Schedule 3). The local education authority designated in the order must be the authority where the child is living or will live, or the authority where the child is a registered pupil at a school (section 36 (7)). It will usually be more appropriate for the former authority to be the designated authority. If a family moves to another area during the currency of an education supervision order, the local education authority designated by it should notify the local education authority to whose area the child is moving and consider with that authority whether to apply to the court for the discharge of the original order and the making of a new order in favour of the receiving authority. This will normally be appropriate unless the original local education authority is the one in whose area the school attended by the child is situated and the child is not changing school.

3.4. Should it be necessary, the local education authority may either institute proceedings under section 39 of the Education Act 1944, whereby the parents of the child may be prosecuted, or apply for an education supervision order, whichever is most likely to be effective in the particular circumstances

3.5. It is important to remember that education supervision order proceedings under section 36 and Schedule 3 are "family proceedings" as defined in section 8(3) and (4) of the Act. This means that when a court is considering an application for an education supervision order, the child's welfare shall be the paramount consideration. In particular the court will have regard to the considerations listed in section 1(3), and it may call for welfare reports and for a hearing to be adjourned for preparation of such reports. The court is required to make an order only if it has grounds to consider that doing so would be better for the child than not doing so. These principles apply when all applications for court orders are made under the Act.

3.6. The court procedures relating to an application for an education supervision order concerning who is to be notified, who are to be parties to the hearing and other matters are determined by Rules of Court made under section 93 of the Act.

GROUNDS FOR APPLYING FOR AN EDUCATION SUPERVISION ORDER

3.7. The effective use of an education supervision order requires commitment, time and skills. Local education authorities will therefore need to review their policies and guidelines to ensure that orders are sought only in appropriate circumstances and that consistent policies are followed within authorities. These policies will need to leave room for flexibility to respond to individual cases, and should encourage effective collaboration between the statutory agencies involved. Local education authorities might consider making their policies on education supervision orders public.

3.8. There may be some situations in which an education supervision order is unlikely to be effective. Where, for example, parents would be hostile to such intervention, it may not be possible to undertake the structured programme of work that is necessary. An alternative strategy will need to be considered in some instances, for example, the use of proceedings under section 39 of the Education Act 1944. As a matter of good practice, an education supervision order should not be sought without the knowledge of the parents.

3.9. An education supervision order could help where parents find it difficult to exercise a proper influence over their child, and where the child has developed a pattern of poor attendance. It would give the backing of the court to the supervising officer and could complement the efforts of the supervising officer to resolve the child's problems by working with the parents to bring them to accept their statutory education responsibilities.

Duty to consult

3.10. When proposing to seek an education supervision order, the local education authority is required by section 36 (8) of the Act to consult the Social Services Committee of the appropriate local authority. Generally consultation will in fact be with a professional officer of the social services department authorised to act as an agent of the Social Services Committee under the usual arrangements for the exercise of delegated authority. Delay can be detrimental to the child's education. Consultation should therefore be completed as quickly as practicable. The outcome should be confirmed in writing, and should indicate whether or not the social services department are involved with the child and/or the family, and if there are any known reasons why an education supervision order would not be appropriate. Whilst it is a requirement to consult, it does not necessarily follow that an agreement will be reached in all circumstances. Where the social services department are already involved they may require the assistance of the local education authority, who are under a duty to comply with the request in accordance with section 27 of the Act, subject to the conditions set out in that section.

Powers and Responsibilities of the Court

3.11. It will be open to the courts, when considering proceedings under section 39 of the Education Act 1944 to direct the local education authority to apply for an education supervision order. In such circumstances, the local education authority will need to consult with the social services department to determine whether it is necessary to make an education supervision order in order to safeguard the child's welfare.

3.12. When the court directs the local education authority to apply for an education supervision order, the local education authority is required to determine whether there are any reasons why it would not be appropriate to make such an application. If the authority intend not to follow the direction of the court, a report outlining their reasons should be presented to the court within eight weeks beginning with the date on which the direction was given (section 40(3), (3A) and 3B) of the Education Act 1944, as amended by the Children Act 1989).

Supervising officer

3.13. The Act does not prescribe the most appropriate supervising officer. This may be an education welfare officer or an education social worker who may already be known to the child and the family, and who is in a good position to deal with any educational issues which arise in such cases. Where it is appropriate and where such an arrangement can be managed effectively, the task may be delegated. If local education authorities use an education welfare officer as a supervising officer or when the task is delegated, they should consider whether the supervising officer is suitably qualified, by training or experience, and can command the confidence of the court. A professional social work qualification as recognised by the Central Council for Education and Training in Social Work would provide one indication that the supervising officer possesses the necessary skills and knowledge. Local education authorities should ensure that they provide capable supervising officers.

3.14 The supervising officer may not always be the same person who was involved with the family prior to an education supervision order being made, and it may also in exceptional circumstances be necessary to change the supervising officer during the course of the order. In the interests of continuity, local education authorities should not make changes without good reasons for doing so. In any circumstances, the allocation of the task is best made on an assessment of the officer most likely to work effectively with the parents and the child. The religious, cultural, racial and linguistic background of the child and the family may also influence the choice of supervising officer.

Reports to the court

3.15. When local education authorities apply for an education supervision order, they should provide the court with a report. That report should relate to the checklist set out in section 1(3) of the Act and should include the following:

(a) the child's record of attendance, distinguishing between justified and unjustified absence. Accurate details of the child's attendance for the twelve school weeks prior to court action being initiated should be provided. It may also be helpful to provide general details of the attendance over a longer period;

(b) relevant details of the child's circumstances including age, sex, background and any particular physical, emotional or educational needs (including special educational needs) the child may have;

(c) an assessment of the causes of the poor attendance of the child (including a medical assessment if relevant) and an indication of the attitudes of the child, the parents, schools and other agencies towards the poor attendance;

(d) a short description of the work that has already been undertaken and its results, giving the reasons why an education supervision order is being requested including an assessment of any likely educational disadvantage to the child should an order not be made;

(e) an outline of the intended intervention, including targets for timing and monitoring. This should include a programme of the intended work, indicating the role of the child, the parents and the school within this work. It should also give an indication of why it is believed that such a programme of work will help to resolve the problem and ensure that the child attends school regularly.

3.16. The report should be prepared in full consultation with both the child and the family. If they disagree with the assessment of the causes of the poor attendance, this should be indicated in the report to the court. The child's welfare is the court's paramount consideration and the report should include relevant information so that the child's needs can be properly assessed together with details of the "checklist" of circumstances and an opinion as to whether an order is itself prejudicial to the child's interests (section 1). It may also be helpful for the court to be supplied with a report from the child's school assessing the educational progress.

3.17. Where there are particular factors relating to the child's religious persuasion, racial origin, or cultural and linguistic background that may have a bearing on the application for the order, or on the manner in which the order is to be conducted, these should be drawn to the attention of the court.

Preparation for an Education Supervision Order

3.18. Before considering applying for an education supervision order, all reasonable efforts should have been made by all the parties to resolve a problem of poor school attendance without the use of legal sanctions. Many attendance difficulties can be overcome by sensitive action by schools and the Education Welfare Service.

3.19. An education supervision order removes from parents rights of appeal against admissions decisions and certain rights to have the child educated in accordance with their wishes. Parents should be made fully aware of this before an order is sought. They should also be made aware of their legal duty to comply with directions made under the order, of the penalties to which they may be liable if they persistently fail to comply with directions (paragraph 18 of Schedule 3), and of their rights of appeal under section 94 of the Act (see paragraph 1.41 below). The child and the family should be told that if the child persistently fails to comply with directions, then the law requires the social services department to investigate the circumstances (paragraph 19 of Schedule 3).

Conduct of an Education Supervisor

3.20. The duties required of the supervising officer are *"to advise, assist, befriend and give directions to"* the child and the parents. The objective is to ensure that the child receives efficient full-time education suitable to his or her age, ability, aptitude and any special educational needs, and that the child benefits fully from the education received. The aim is to establish and strengthen parental responsibility, and to enable the parents to discharge their responsibility towards the child. There is no specified amount of contact between the supervising officer and the parents and the child. Thus, the amount of contact that is necessary will be determined by the need to achieve the original aims and objectives.

3.21. To undertake such a programme of work, the supervising officer should exercise a range of skills and techniques. The supervising officer should have good insight and understanding of family behaviour. Knowledge of counselling and guidance techniques may be needed to help change patterns of behaviour which may be undermining the ability of the child to benefit from education. The supervising officer should be sensitive to the educational needs of the child and be able to act in that regard in cooperation with the school, on behalf of the child and the parents.

3.22. Much of the work is likely to involve the child, the parents and the school in order to establish a relationship that will strengthen the parents' ability and commitment to discharge their responsibilities. The local education authority should therefore not neglect any of the parties involved. At times, it may be helpful to counsel the child to help identify ways that education may be more beneficial. However, work with the child alone will not, in itself, enable the parents to resolve difficulties the child is experiencing. The supervising officer should always have in mind the need to establish, reinforce and maintain parental authority and should aim to support parents in communicating effectively with the child.

3.23. At all times the supervising officer will need to operate within a structure that defines clear aims and objectives. This will require a planned and realistic programme of intervention, including directions where necessary, which will specify how the aims and objectives are to be achieved. The active involvement of parents, children and schools will aid success.

3.24. The supervising officer will need adequate back-up and assistance from the local education authority. Efficient recording and information systems will assist effective working. Authorities will need to consider the extent to which they need to review and revise current procedures.

3.25. The progress of an education supervision order needs to be subject to regular review in order to establish that the intervention is achieving the intended result. This should take place within regular discussion between supervising officers and their managers. Wherever intended aims and objectives are not being met, it is essential to act promptly to explore alternative strategies. Authorities will need to ensure that their systems are appropriate for evaluating the effectiveness of education supervision orders.

3.26. It is important for the supervising officer to be sensitive to the educational needs of the child. Where it is apparent that these are not being met, it may be necessary to establish whether the child has any special educational needs as defined in the Education Act 1981. The supervising officer needs to be alert to these issues and should be able to recommend an assessment and review under that Act, if that is necessary.

3.27. Supervising officers will need to keep in mind that, under section 36 of the Education Act 1944, parents have the right to educate their children of compulsory school age other than in school provided that they can satisfy their local education authority that they are providing efficient full-time education suitable for the child's age, ability, aptitude and special educational needs. In addition, local education authorities are empowered in certain circumstances to take the initiative in arranging education otherwise than at school for children of compulsory school age (section 56 of the Education Act 1944)

3.28. Supervising officers will need to work closely with schools. They may also find it helpful to turn to other sources for help in their task. Social services departments and other agencies may have established programmes that could benefit the child and the parents.

3.29. Section 31 of the Act provides for the making of care orders and supervision orders. Where it appears to the supervising officer that sufficient grounds exist for the making of a care order or a supervision order on a child who is subject to an education supervision order, then this matter should be discussed between the local education authority and the social services department. It may be that the social services department can help with the provision of services under Part III and Part I of Schedule 2 of the Act which would make court proceedings unnecessary.

Change of school

3.30. Under paragraph 13 of Schedule 3 to the Act, parents lose their right to have the child educated in accordance with their wishes while an education supervision order is in force. They no longer have the right to move their child to another school and have no right of appeal against admissions decisions. It may be, however, that a change of school could be of benefit to the child, and the supervising officer should be sensitive to such matters and ready to act on behalf of the child. The parents' temporary loss of rights in this matter need not prevent a change of educational provision should it be necessary. Nor should the loss of parents' rights prevent discussion with them about the arrangements for the education of their child.

The Use of Directions

3.31. Paragraph 12 of Schedule 3 empowers the supervising officer to give directions to the supervised child or the parent. The supervisor is duty bound to consider the wishes and feelings of the child and parents (paragraphs 12(2) and 12(3) of Schedule 3) and to ensure that the directions are reasonable. Supervisors should keep in mind that it is a defence in the case of prosecution if parents can show that directions were unreasonable (paragraph 18(2)(b) of Schedule 3).

3.32. Directions might include, for example, a requirement for the parents and the child to attend meetings with the supervisor or with teachers at the school to discuss the child's progress. They may need to cover such areas as medical treatment or examination, or assessment by an educational psychologist.

3.33. Directions need to be made with care. Whilst the authority of the supervisor needs to be respected, that authority should be exercised with tact, caution and thought. It is also important that directions are used only where necessary.

3.34. Directions should be confirmed in writing, and where a child is being given a direction the parents also need to be told of this in writing. Written confirmation could be given at the same time as the direction is explained to the parent or child.

3.35. If parents fail to comply with a reasonable direction, they need to be told in writing that under an education supervision order they are required to follow the directions of the supervising officer and that they may be guilty of an offence if they persistently fail to comply.

Compliance with Directions

3.36. The supervising officer has a vital role to play in ensuring that education supervision orders operate effectively in dealing with the education problem that has been identified. Where parents *persistently* fail to comply with directions, and those directions are reasonable, they may be guilty of an offence. In such circumstances, the supervising officer must ensure that the matter is drawn to the attention of the court. Upon conviction, the parents will be liable to a fine not exceeding level 3 on the standard scale.

3.37. Where a parent or a child persistently fails to comply with a direction given under the order, the supervising officer should ensure that the social services department is informed. In such cases, the department must investigate the circumstances, of the child and consider whether it is appropriate for them to take any action to secure the welfare of the child (paragraph 19 of Schedule 3). In doing so, they may need to seek the views of other support services, but they should not lose sight of the need to move quickly so as to bring about real improvement. If it is clear that improvements in attendance are not being achieved, the social services department has a duty to consider seeking a care order under section 31 of the Act, following the criteria laid down in section 1 (see paragraph 1.5 above).

Ceasing or extending an Order

3.38. An order will normally cease to be effective after one year or when the child is no longer of compulsory school age (paragraph 15 of Schedule 3). However, the court may discharge the order before that time on the application of the child, the parents or the local education authority (paragraph 17(1) of Schedule 3).

3.39. The supervising officer may seek the discharge because the objectives of the order have been met before the completion of a full year. This may be because the child is in receipt of efficient full-time education and there is good reason to believe that the parents are able to ensure that this is likely to continue for the foreseeable future.

3.40. An education supervision order may be extended for up to three years if an application is made by the authority not earlier than three months before the expiry date, and the order may be extended on more than one occasion (paragraph 15 of Schedule 3). Such an extension may be sought where the supervising officer feels it necessary to ensure the continuing progress of the child's education.

3.41. Under section 94 of the Act, parents have a right of appeal to the High Court against the making of an order.

Child subject to a Supervision Order or a Criminal Supervision Order

3.42. A child who is the subject of an education supervision order may also be the subject of a supervision order to a social services department or a criminal supervision order made under section 7(7)(b) of the Children and Young Persons Act 1969.

3.43. There are similar aspects to the orders, but the education supervision order is specifically concerned with ensuring that the child receives an adequate education. If there are different supervising officers, it will be necessary for them to co-ordinate their efforts and to develop a clear understanding of their respective roles. There may well be scope for cooperative work; and it will be necessary to maintain good lines of communication, and to ensure that the parents and the child are fully aware of the different roles of the two supervising officers. Failure to comply with a direction under an education supervision order is to be disregarded if it would not have been reasonably practicable to comply with it without failing to comply with a direction given under another order (paragraph 14 of Schedule 3).

Duties of Social Services Departments in relation to Education Departments and Education Supervision Orders

3.44. The social services department may be required to investigate the circumstances of a child when an education supervision order is discharged, or where a child persistently fails to comply with the directions of the supervising officer (paragraphs 17(2) and 19(2) of Schedule 3). If this is required, the social services department must consider whether it would be appropriate to initiate proceedings under section 31 or to provide services under Part III.

Conclusion

3.45. The aim of the new provision is to provide an effective means of guiding parents and children so as to ensure that all children receive a satisfactory education. Supervisors are responsible for ensuring that an education supervision order brings about the required improvement, and for taking further action in the event that it fails to do so. In doing so, they need to keep in mind the best interests of the child, the requirements of the law on school attendance, and their responsibility to the court for the effective discharge of the order.

3.46. Education supervision orders provide a new means of ensuring that school age children benefit from an effective education. They give to local education authorities the opportunity for a change of direction and of emphasis. The new procedures which they will require will not represent a substantial new burden on authorities. Many of the changes will replace current practices rather than add to them, and there is plenty of scope for deploying existing resources in more effective ways to meet the new situation. Local education authorities will need to consider building on existing practices to adopt new approaches and priorities to meet the challenges of education supervision orders.

CHAPTER 4 TRANSFER OF CARE ORDERS AND RECOVERY OF CHILDREN

INTRODUCTION

4.1. The Prescribed Orders - Northern Ireland, Guernsey and Isle of Man Regulations (reproduced at Annex C) are made under section 101 of the Children Act 1989. They provide for:–

(a) the transfer of care of children who are to live outside the country in which their care or equivalent orders were made;

(b) the recovery of children to whom section 50 of the Act applies who have absconded, been abducted or unlawfully kept away from the responsible person as defined in section 49 of the Act or are missing.

TRANSFER OF CARE ORDERS

Transfer of Care Orders from England and Wales to Northern Ireland

4.2. Regulation 2 provides for the transfer of responsibility for the care of children who are the subject of care orders under section 31 of the Act who move from England or Wales to live in Northern Ireland. It applies where a court has given its approval (under paragraph 19(1) of Schedule 2 to the Act) to the local authority in arranging or assisting to arrange for the child to live outside its home area. The transfer of criminal supervision orders with a condition of residence under section 12AA of the Children and Young Persons Act 1969, and for a transitional period of six months from 14th October 1991 criminal care orders, will continue to be possible under section 25(2) of the 1969 Act. However, it should be noted that such supervision orders can only last for six months and criminal care orders cannot exist beyond 13th April 1992.

4.3. Where this Regulation applies the care order ceases to have effect and the child is treated as if he had been committed to the care of the Board for the area in which it is proposed that he will live in Northern Ireland.

Transfer of Care Orders from Northern Ireland to England and Wales

4.4. Until such time as court - based transfers are possible in Northern Ireland, ie when the Northern Ireland Children Order is made and brought into operation, the transfer of responsibility for the care of children in Northern Ireland who are the subject of fit person orders and training school orders to England or Wales will continue to be effected under section 25(1) of the Children and Young Persons Act 1969.

Transfer of Care Orders to/from Isle of Man and England and Wales

4.5. Regulations 3 and 4 provide for the transfer of responsibility for the care of children who are the subject of prescribed orders within the meaning of these Regulations who move between England and Wales and the Isle of Man. They apply where a court has given its approval to the appropriate authority in arranging or assisting to arrange for the child to live outside its home area. Orders made on a finding of guilt will still be able to be transferred in accordance with section 26 of the 1969 Act.

4.6. Where a relevant order within the meaning of section 56(6) of the Children and Young Persons Act 1966 (an Act of Tynwald) is transferred under Regulation 3 it shall *not* cease to have effect in the Isle of Man.

4.7. Where a care order is transferred to the Isle of Man under Regulation 4 it shall cease to have effect in England and Wales by virtue of section 101(4) of the Children Act 1989.

Transfer of Care Orders from England and Wales to Guernsey

4.8. Regulation 5 provides for the transfer of responsibility for the care of children who are the subject of care orders under section 31 of the Act who move from England or Wales to live in Guernsey. It applies:–

(a) where a court has given its approval (under paragraph 19(1) of Schedule 2 to the Act) to the local authority in arranging or assisting to arrange for a child to live outside its home area;

(b) the States Children Board in Guernsey has notified the Guernsey Juvenile Court that it agrees to receive the child into its care and the local authority on the mainland has notified the Court that it is agreeable to this;

(c) the Guernsey Juvenile Court has made a fit person order in respect of the child.

4.9. Where this Regulation applies the care order ceases to have affect and the child is treated as if he had been committed to the care of the States Children Board.

Transfer of Care Orders from England and Wales to Jersey

4.10. There is currently no provision for the transfer of Care Orders from the mainland to Jersey.

Transfer of Care Orders from the Channel Islands to England and Wales

4.11. Such transfers will continue to be effected under section 26 of the Children and Young Persons Act 1969.

4.12. These Regulations do not apply to any orders made on a finding of guilt in England or Wales or elsewhere. Where appropriate such cases will continue to be transferred under section 26 of the Children and Young Persons Act 1969.

RECOVERY ORDERS

4.13. Recovery orders may only be made in respect of children who are in care or are the subject of an emergency protection order or are in police protection.

4.14. A court may make a recovery order under section 50 of the Act if it has reason to believe that the child:–

(a) has been unlawfully taken away or is being unlawfully kept away from the responsible person, ie any person who for the time being has care of the child by virtue of a care order, an emergency protection order or section 46 of the Act;

(b) has run away or is staying away from the responsible person; or

(c) is missing.

4.15. A recovery order:–

(a) operates as a direction to any person who is in a position to do so to produce the child on request to any authorised person (within the meaning of section 50(7) of the Act);

(b) authorises the removal of the child by any authorised person;

(c) requires any person who has information as to the child's whereabouts to disclose that information, if asked to do so, to a constable or an officer of the court;

(d) authorises a constable to enter any premises specified in the order and search for the child, using reasonable force if necessary.

Transfer of Recovery Orders from England and Wales to Northern Ireland

4.16. Regulation 6 provides for the recovery of children to whom paragraph 4.13 applies who are taken from England and Wales to Northern Ireland. A recovery order made by a court in England and Wales shall have effect for the purposes of the law in Northern Ireland as if it had been made by a magistrates' court within the meaning of the Magistrates' Courts (Northern Ireland) Order 1981.

4.17. Any reasonable expenses incurred by an authorised person effecting a recovery order under Regulation 6 shall be recoverable from the authority in whose care the child was.

Transfer of Recovery Orders from Northern Ireland to the United Kingdom and Channel Islands

4.18. Until such time as the Northern Ireland Children Order is made and comes into operation the recovery of Northern Ireland Children in care from the United Kingdom or the Channel Islands will continue to be effected under section 32(1) of the Children and Young Persons Act 1969.

Transfer of Recovery Orders to England and Wales from the Isle of Man

4.19. Regulation 7 provides for the recovery of children to whom paragraph 4.13 applies who are taken from the Isle of Man to England or Wales except that it shall not apply to a child in care by virtue of an order on a finding of guilt.

Transfer of Recovery Orders from England and Wales to the Isle of Man

4.20. Section 98C of the Children and Young Persons Act 1966 (an Act of Tynwald) provides for the recovery of children to whom paragraph 4.13 applies who are taken to the Isle of Man from England or Wales.

Transfer of Recovery Orders to/from England and Wales and the Channel Islands

4.21. There is currently no provision for a court based recovery of children to whom paragraph 4.13 applies who are taken from England and Wales to the Channel Islands and vice versa.

CHAPTER 5 SECURE ACCOMMODATION

SECURE ACCOMMODATION ORDERS

5.1. The guidance on secure accommodation orders in Chapter 5 of Volume 1 (Court Orders) in this series of Regulations and Guidance was prepared when the Secure Accommodation Regulations were still in draft form. Because of subsequent changes to the draft regulations some references are no longer correct. A copy of the Children (Secure Accommodation) Regulations 1991 (SI No. 1505) is included as Annex G to Volume 4 (Residential Care) in this series of Regulations and Guidance and a full explanation of their purpose is described in Chapter 8 of that Volume.

The Children (Secure Accommodation)(No.2) Regulations 1991

5.2. Chapter 8 of Volume 4 in this series of Regulations and Guidance (Residential Care) described the statutory framework in section 25 of the Act governing restriction of liberty and the further provisions included in the Children (Secure Accommodation) Regulations 1991. In particular, paragraphs 8.13–8.17 described the arrangements for extending the statutory safeguards governing restriction of liberty to children accommodated by health authorities (including National Health Service Trusts) and local education authorities. Similarly, paragraphs 8.18–8.21 described the extension of the statutory safeguards to children accommodated in residential care homes, nursing homes and mental nursing homes.

5.3. As foreshadowed in that guidance, further regulations have now been made to enable the bodies described above to make application to the court to place or keep a child in secure accommodation (the Children (Secure Accommodation)(No.2) Regulations 1991 – see Annex D).

5.4. The sole purpose and effect of the (No. 2) Regulations is to enable health authorities (including National Health Service Trusts) and local education authorities, and those carrying on residential care homes, nursing homes and mental nursing homes to make application to the court under section 25 of the 1989 Act for authority to restrict the liberty of a child they are providing with accommodation. However, if such a child is looked after by a local authority within the meaning of section 22(1) of the Act, responsibility for making application to the court remains with that authority. In making application to the court for authority to restrict liberty it will be for the health or education authority, or those carrying on the relevant home as the case may be, to produce adequate evidence to the court to support their view that the specific statutory criteria for restriction of liberty in section 25(1) apply in the particular case.

Power of courts to deal with applications to restrict liberty under section 25 of the 1989 Act in criminal proceedings

5.5. The opportunity has been taken in the Criminal Justice Act 1991 to correct a small anomaly in section 92(2) the Children Act 1989. That section specifies that proceedings under the 1989 Act *"shall be treated as family proceedings in relation to magistrates' courts"*. As such, all applications for authority to restrict liberty under section 25 of the Act would fall to be dealt with as civil proceedings. However, this would not be appropriate where an application to restrict liberty was connected with the appearance of a child before a court in criminal proceedings. The intention was that that latter court should also have power to authorise restriction of liberty. The position has now been corrected by section 60(3) of the Criminal Justice Act 1991. This says that *"in the case of a child or young person who has been remanded or committed to local authority accommodation by a youth court or a magistrates' court other than a youth court, any application under section 25 of the Children Act 1989 shall, notwithstanding anything in section 92(2) of that Act or section 65 of the 1980 (Magistrates' Courts) Act, be made to that court."* It should be noted that the power to consider applications under section 25 does not extend to the Crown Court. When a juvenile is remanded to appear before the Crown Court for trial or sentence it will be necessary for applications for orders under section 25 to continue to be made to a youth court or a magistrates' court other than a youth court. Guidance about the maximum duration of court authority to restrict liberty in remand cases is given in paragraph 8.46 of Volume 4 (Residential Care) in this series of Regulations and Guidance. Arrangements are being made for section 60(3) of the Criminal Justice Act 1991 to be brought into force on the same date as the implementation of the 1989 Act.

5.6. It should be noted that the guidance given in paragraph 8.4 of Volume 4 in this series of Regulations and Guidance (Residential Care) dealing with the jurisdiction of courts in considering applications under section 25 of the Act already reflects the position described above.

CHAPTER 6 TRANSITIONAL ARRANGEMENTS

INTRODUCTION

6.1. This guidance seeks to expand on the contents and effect of Schedule 14 (Transitionals and Savings) of the Children Act. The Schedule has been amended by the Courts and Legal Services Act (see Annex G), the Children Act 1989 (Commencement and Transitional Provisions) Order 1991 (SI No 1991/828) (reproduced at Annex E) and the further transitional provisions contained in the Children Act 1989 (Commencement No. 2 – Amendment and Transitional Provisions) Order (SI No 1991/1990) (reproduced at Annex F).

6.2. The guidance is intended primarily as a checklist for action that may be required either before or after implementation and as an aid. Definitive interpretation of legal provisions can necessarily only be provided by the Courts. The guidance focuses on public law orders and surrounding issues, commenting on private law concerns only where they appear relevant to local authorities.

Pending Proceedings

6.3. These will cover nearly all cases where proceedings have been commenced, even though there has not yet been a court hearing. They will include wardship proceedings (subject to the comments below), and also cases where an appeal has been lodged, or time to appeal has not yet expired (as for example an appeal against the making of an administrative parental rights resolution).

6.4. In all pending proceedings the case will continue as if the 1989 Act did not exist, until a final order is made. Such an order will then be deemed to be an order in force immediately before the commencement of the Act and the appropriate transitional arrangements will apply (see below). The order will not, however, be backdated, so that for example where a final care order is made on 14 November 1991, it will be deemed to be a new care order under the Act as of that date.

6.5. Depending on the date proceedings were instituted and the stage reached prior to commencement of the Act, local authorities will wish to consider whether to carry on with the existing proceedings or whether to withdraw their application and initiate new proceedings under the new jurisdiction.

6.6. Exceptions to the 'pending' provision are proceedings under the Matrimonial Causes Act 1973 (section 42(3)) and the Sexual Offences Act 1956 (Section 38). These will cease to have effect as parents always retain parental responsibility (section 2(1)). For the same reason an order already in existence under these enactments will, on commencement of the Act, cease to have effect. The local authority will need to consider whether there are any child protection issues at stake and take appropriate action.

Family Law Reform Act 1987 (section 4(1))

6.7. An order under the Family Law Reform Act 1987 which gives a father parental rights and duties where the parents are not married to each other is deemed, on commencement of the Children Act, to be a parental responsibility order. Since this transitional arrangement refers to a putative father who had rights and duties *immediately* before commencement of the Act, it does not come into effect on the revocation of a freeing order under section 20(3) of the Adoption Act 1976 (as substituted by paragraph 8 of schedule 10 to the 1989 Act). Where a putative father had rights and duties prior to, the making of an order freeing the child for adoption and the freeing order is subsequently revoked, the putative father will need to apply to the court, or obtain the agreement of the mother, for parental responsibility.

Custody and Care and Control Orders

6.8. Provisions relating to existing custody and care and control orders contained in paragraphs 6–11 of Schedule 14 do *not* apply to care and control orders made in wardship proceedings, where responsibility for the child is vested in the court.

6.9. Under section 33 of the Children Act 1975 a custodianship order effectively suspended the parental responsibility of the parents. On commencement of the Act, custodianship orders are deemed to be parental responsibility orders where the parental responsibility is shared with the parents. Local authorities will need to discuss the implications of this with any local authority foster parent who has a custodianship order in his or her favour.

6.10. The transitional provision in SI 1991/1990 enables local authority allowances currently paid to custodians under the Children Act 1975 (section 34(6)) to continue to be paid for as long as the order lasts, even though the whole of that Act has been repealed.

Children in Care

6.11. All children -

(a) in care by virtue of a care order under specified provisions;

(b) in care by virtue of an order, the effect of which is as though the child had been received into care, such as an order under section 2(1)(e) of the Matrimonial Proceedings (Magistrates' Court Act) 1960;

(c) "in care" under specified provisions;

(d) in care in wardship proceedings by virtue of a *final* order made in the exercise of the High Court's inherent jurisdiction or pursuant to section 7(2) of the Family Law Reform Act 1969 (but see below),

are deemed to be in the care of the same local authority under section 31 of the Act.

6.12. Interim care orders made under section 2(10) of the Children & Young Persons Act 1969, however, are *not* covered by these arrangements. They will be regarded as orders made in pending proceedings, and issues concerning.contact (access) and applications for any further interim order will be considered under the old jurisdiction.

6.13. The Children Act 1989 (Commencement No. 2 – Amendment and Transitional Provisions) Order 1991 (SI 1991/1990) amends the transitional provisions contained in the Courts and Legal Services Act (paragraph 33 of schedule 16 and SI 1991/828) relating to care and control orders (interim orders) made in wardship proceedings. These orders are deemed to be pending proceedings for a maximum period of twelve months from commencement of the Act (unless disposed of sooner) during which time the wardship continues (regardless of the provisions of paragraph 16A of Schedule 14). Such proceedings should be brought back to court at the earliest opportunity (consistent with the best interests of the child) and if a final care order is made under section 7(2) of the Family Law Reform Act 1969, or in the exercise of the High Court's inherent jurisdiction, this will become a care order under the Act and the wardship will cease. Any outstanding care and control orders on 14 October 1992 will convert to full care orders under the Act and the wardship will cease from that date.

6.14. In the light of these transitional arrangements, local authorities will need to amend their records to ensure the child's correct legal status is noted and consider whether or not to apply to discharge or vary the order where the circumstances of the case and the welfare of the child suggest that this and particularly lesser intervention would be appropriate.

6.15. The implications of these provisions where a care order is deemed to be made include:

Access and contact

(i) The provisions of the 1989 Act will apply. This means, for example, there will be a presumption that contact will be allowed with parents (see section 34). Contact cannot generally be refused without a court order except in an emergency for a maximum of 7 days.

Where there is already a section 12C Child Care Act 1980 access order in force immediately before 14 October 1991, it will be treated as if it was a section 34 order in favour of the person named in the order (paragraph 18 of Schedule 14).

Where a notice has been given under section 12B to terminate access or refuse to make arrangements for access, this will have effect as a court order under section 34(4) refusing to allow contact between the child and the person to whom notice had been given (paragraph 5 of the Schedule to SI 1991/828). The person named may, of course, then apply to the court for the order to be varied or discharged under section 34 of the Act. It is not intended in these circumstances that section 91(17) will apply, which requires the leave of the court if an appeal is to be heard within six months of the final decision. That section refers to applications that have been refused and not to orders that are deemed to have been made.

Where an access order under section 12C has been suspended in an emergency situation under section 12E, the suspending order shall continue as if the 1989 Act had not been passed unless the authority applied to vary or discharge it before 14 October 1991, in which case it continues until that application has been decided. Once an order had been varied, it would have effect as a section 34 order. Local authorities should consider applying for an order under section 34 if they wish to maintain a restricted contact regime after the Act comes into force.

Consultation

(ii) Not only a child in care has the right to be consulted about any decision relating to him so far as practicable (section 22(4)), but so also do his parents and anyone else the authority considers relevant. The authority must also consider the child's religious persuasion, racial origin and cultural and linguistic background (section 22(5)).

Secure Accommodation

(iii) The new provisions about secure accommodation will apply (section 25).

Review Regulations

(iv) The child's care must be reviewed at intervals specified in the Review of Children's Cases Regulations 1991 (see also the Children (Representations, Placements and Reviews) (Miscellaneous Amendments) Regulations 1991 – reproduced at Annex M).

Complaints Procedure

(v) The child, his parents, local authority foster parents (and others specified in section 26(3)) will have access to a new complaints procedure with an independent element, and the opportunity to appear before a panel, also including an independent person.

Advise, Assist and Befriend

(vi) Young persons who cease to be looked after by the local authority after reaching their 16th birthday will qualify for advice and assistance until their 21st birthday. Aftercare provision will need to be developed for young people due to leave care or accommodation, and for those who may already have left when aged 16 or over and have yet to reach their 21st birthday.

Directions and Injunctions

6.16. Although an old style care order will be deemed to be a new one, if the court gave directions when making the care order (whether by the two specified statutes* or by virtue of its inherent jurisdiction) as for example freeing for adoption or termination of access, those directions shall continue to have effect until varied or discharged by the court that made them (paragraph 16(5) of Schedule 14 to the 1989 Act and the Children (Allocation of Proceedings) Order 1991). This is so despite any provision in the 1989 Act to the contrary, except that it is subject to the secure accommodation provisions in section 25 and regulations made under it (paragraph 3 of the Schedule to SI 1991/828). In particular, where directions have authorised restricting the child's liberty, those directions shall expire at the end of 3 months from 14 October 1991, although a court could extend them for further periods of 6 months in accordance with the Secure Accommodation Regulations (Children (Secure Accommodation) Regulations 1991 and Children (Secure Accommodation) (No. 2) Regulations 1991 – the latter are not relevant to these transitional provisions).

6.17. As soon after commencement of the Act as is reasonably practicable local authorities should consider, as part of their assessment of all orders made in their favour, whether to seek a discharge or variation of these directions. This will be particularly relevant where the directions may no longer be appropriate or in the child's interests.

6.18. Where a local authority initiated wardship proceedings prior to the commencement of the Act solely for the purpose of obtaining an injunction the injunction will remain live until varied or discharged. Similarly any injunction granted where a child is a ward of court and in care by virtue of a final order under a specified statute or in the exercise of the High Court's inherent jurisdiction will remain in force until varied or discharged, even though the care order is deemed a care order under the Act and the wardship ceases. Action for breach of the injunction will be heard in the High Court that made the order.

Wardship

6.19. Where a child is a ward of court and, in proceedings that are not pending, is in care pursuant to section 7(2) of the Family Law Reform Act 1969, or in the exercise of the court's inherent jurisdiction, the wardship will cease on 14 October 1991. The child will be deemed to be in care under a new care order. Any directions which the wardship made will continue subject to the general rules about directions.

6.20. Where a child is in care in wardship under an interim order, one year from the date of commencement of the Act, the proceedings will no longer be deemed to be pending. The order will convert to a full care order (SI 1991/1990) and the wardship will cease.

6.21. Similarly if a child is in care under the 1969 Act and is then made a ward of court before 14 October 1991, the wardship will cease on 14 October 1991.

6.22. If the child is a ward but not in care on 14 October 1991, and a care order is subsequently made, the wardship ceases when the care order is made (section 91(4)).

*Section 43(5)(a) of the Matrimonial Causes Act 1973 and section 4(4)(a) of the Guardianship Act 1973.

Placement with Parents

6.23. Where a child is deemed to be in the care of a local authority and immediately before 14 October 1991 the child was in the charge and control of a parent (or a person in whose favour an order was made under, for example, the Matrimonial Causes Act 1973), the placement shall be deemed to comply with section 23(5) and the Placement of Children with Parents etc Regulations 1991.

Children in Voluntary Care

6.24. Where before 14 October 1991, the child was in care, for example, because his parents were not able to look after him for some reason, he shall be treated after 14 October 1991 as being accommodated, by the authority under Part III of the Act so long as he remains in such accommodation. This does not apply to children who have been abandoned or require permanent care where the authority has resolved to vest parental rights in itself. It also does not apply to cases where the authority has given care and control to the parent or guardian.

6.25. The implications of Part III applying include–

(a) the case will be subject to regular review under section 26,

(b) the complaints procedure under section 26 will apply,

(c) there will be a a duty to promote contact with the parents (para 15 of Schedule 2) etc.

(d) the child will qualify for advice and assistance until his/her 21st birthday (section 24)

Boarded-out Children

6.26. Where a child was in voluntary care and boarded-out or under the charge and control of a relative or friend (but not with a parent or guardian, or under an order listed in paragraph 5 of Schedule 14, for example, custody under the Matrimonial Causes Act 1973), he shall be deemed to be in the care of a local authority foster parent for as long as he remains with such a person. The foster parent will not be subject to the Foster Placement (Children) Regulations 1991 for the period of 12 months after 14 October 1991. Until then, the placement is subject to section 21 of the Child Care Act 1980 and the Boarding-Out of Children (Foster Placement) Regulations 1988. The main difference with the new regulations is that they approve the foster parent rather than the household, and local authority responsibilities in respect of children placed by voluntary organisations are enhanced.

6.27. When a child is deemed to be in care and who was immediately prior to the commencement of the Act in the charge and control of a parent, guardian or person who has previously had care and control of the child under an order listed in paragraph 5 of Schedule 14 (but is, for example, a relative or friend), the placement with Parents etc Regulations 1991 shall apply. Local authorities will not be required to comply with pre-placement action but will have to comply with the Regulations post- placement to the extent that they have not already been complied with.

Arrangements for Placement of Children (General) Regulations 1991

6.28. For children who are in the care of a local authority or accommodated by a voluntary organisation or in a registered children's home on the day before the Act comes into force, all relevant requirements of the Arrangements for Placement Regulations should apply from the day on which the Act comes into force in so far as is practicable. These Regulations will also apply to respite care placements. The first review (under the Review of Children's Cases Regulations) after implementation of the Act should be used to check that the requirements of these regulations are met, such as written agreements and arrangements, and notifications to the extent that these `have not already taken place.

Reviews of Children's Cases

6.29. The Children (Representations, Placements and Reviews) (Miscellaneous Amendments) Regulations 1991 (Annex M) provide for the following transitional arrangements where a child has been accommodated by a local authority, voluntary organisation or registered children's home immediately before 14 October 1991.

6.30. Where a child has been accommodated by a local authority, voluntary organisation or in a registered children's home for less than 4 weeks before 14 October 1991 and–

(a) there has not been a review, the review should be carried out within 4 weeks of 14 October. Thereafter, reviews should be carried out in accordance with Regulation 3(2) of the Review of Children's Cases Regulations 1991;

(b) there has been a review before 14 October, the case should be reviewed thereafter in accordance with Regulation 3(2) of the Review of Children's Cases Regulations 1991.

6.31. Where the child has been accommodated by a local authority, voluntary organisation or in a registered children's home for four weeks or more but for less than 3 months before 14 October and–

(a) there has not been a review of the case, the review should be carried out within 3 months of 14 October. Thereafter, reviews should be carried out not more than six months before the date of the previous review;

(b) there has been a review before 14 October, the case should be reviewed thereafter not more than six months after the date of the previous review.

6.32. Where the child has been accommodated by a local authority, voluntary organisation or in a registered children's home for three months or more, but for less than six months before 14 October 1991 and–

(a) there has not been a review of the case, the review should be carried out within six months of the day on which the child was first so accommodated. Thereafter, reviews should be carried out not more than six months after the date of the previous review;

(b) there has been a review of the case before 14 October, the case should be reviewed thereafter not more than six months after the date of the previous review.

6.33. Where the child has been accommodated in a registered children's home other than by a local authority or voluntary organisation for more than six months before 14 October 1991, a review should be carried out within six months of 14 October. Thereafter, reviews should be carried out not more than six months after the date of the previous review.

6.34. Paragraphs 6.30 and 6.31 above cover those cases where a child was accommodated before 14 October, whether or not a review has taken place. The aim is to bring reviews into the required cycle in a staged process so as to allow for practicable arrangements.

6.35. Paragraph 6.32 above deals with cases where a review may have already taken place under section 27(4) of the Children and Young Persons Act 1969 and should have taken place in any event within six months from the date on which the child was first accommodated. Therefore, the requirement is for the first review after 14 October to take place within six months of the date on which the child was accommodated, *not six months from the 14 October.*

6.36. The requirement in paragraph 6.33 above makes allowance for the fact that prior to 14 October there was not requirement on registered children's' homes to hold reviews (which includes independent schools with 50 or fewer boarders and not approved for special education under section 11(3)(a) of the Education Act 1981). A longer time is allowed for bringing these cases into the required review cycle as there may need to be more work done to set up the review process in such cases.

6.37. Section 17 of the Interpretation Act 1978 covers cases where the child has been accommodated by a local authority or voluntary organisation for more than six months before 14 October 1991. In these cases reviews should continue at six monthly intervals. Section 17 provides that any provision not repealed or re-enacted with or without modification continues to apply. Therefore, a review cycle under section 27(4) of the Children and Young persons Act 1969 continues to apply and provides continuity in the review process. Where there has not been a review of the case, the review should be carried out within six months of the day on which the child was first so accommodated. Thereafter, whether or not there has been a review before 14 October, in a case in which a child was accommodated for more than 6 months on 14 October and where 6 monthly reviews have taken place, reviews should continue to take place at intervals of no more than 6 months.

Representations Procedure Regulations 1991

6.38. The Regulations will not apply to representations received before 14 October 1991. Until then the Community Care Complaints Procedure Directions 1990 will apply to all representations/ complaints. After 14 October those Directions will continue to apply to those representations/complaints not covered by the Children Act procedure.

Emigration of Children in Care

6.39. Where there is an outstanding application for the Secretary of State's consent to the emigration of a child in care with the Department on 14 October 1991, section 24 of the Child Care Act 1980 will continue to apply as though it had not been repealed until the Secretary of State makes a decision on the application.

Contribution towards the Maintenance of Children looked after by Local authorities

6.40. Paragraph 24 of Schedule 14 refers to various enactments by which either parent may be required to pay maintenance for a child in care. Under the transitional arrangements such maintenance payments are converted to contribution orders (Schedule 2 paragraph 23(2)). Although no provisions are set out for similar payments made under the Child Care Act 1980 (section 47) section 16 of the Interpretation Act 1978 provides that where an Act is repealed, unless there is a clear contrary intention, the repeal will not affect liabilities already incurred under the old Act. Accordingly, the old orders will continue unaffected.

Liability to Contribute

6.41. Local authorities are required by paragraph 21(1)-(3) of Schedule 2 to consider whether it is reasonable to recover contributions towards the maintenance of a child they are looking after from his parents or, if the child is aged 16 or over, from the child himself. Paragraph 21(4) of Schedule 2 exempts parents from being liable to make contributions if they are in receipt of Income Support or Family Credit. There is an unintentional omission in not referring also to the child aged 16 or over in receipt of these benefits as also being exempt from contributing. This omission will be corrected by amending primary legislation at the earliest suitable opportunity. Until this is done, local authorities should follow the guidance in paragraph 2.40 of Volume 2 in the Children Act series of Guidance and Regulations which has been written as though the omission had already been corrected.

Supervision Orders made under section 1(3)(b) of the Children and Young Persons Act 1969 or section 21(2) of that Act on the discharge of a care order under section 1(3)(c) of that Act

6.42. These will be deemed to be made under section 31 of the Act. If there is a requirement for the child to reside with a named person, this will remain for as long as the order is in force, unless the court directs otherwise. Any other requirements of the court, or directions given by the supervisor, will be deemed to have been made under Schedule 3.

6.43. A new supervision order normally lasts for up to 12 months. Transitionally, if the order had been in force on 13 October 1991 for 6 months or more, it will cease to have effect at the end of 6 months beginning with 14 October 1991 unless it ceases to have effect earlier because a care order is made (see section 91(3)), or it would have expired earlier were it not for the Act, or the court directs otherwise (but this must not exceed 3 years and it is intended that the 3 year period runs from the date the order was first made). If the order had been in force for less than 6 months, it will run for a year from 14 October 1991 subject to the same provisions as above. The local authority will wish to consider what, if any, further alternative action is required. If an extension is sought the application will have to be made to the court *after* the date of commencement of the Act but *before* the date on which the order would otherwise have expired. Where the local authority wish to obtain a care order in place of the supervision order it must first satisfy the court of the preconditions under section 31.

Most other Supervision Orders

6.44. These include section 44 of the Matrimonial Causes Act (court appoints independent person to supervise child in exceptional circumstances) and section 7(4) of the Family Law Reform Act 1969 (exceptionally, a ward of court can be made subject to the supervision of an independent person). These are not deemed to be section 31 orders, but shall continue in force for a year from 14 October 1991 unless the order would anyway have ended earlier, or the court directs that it should end earlier. Again the local authority will wish to consider what further action should be taken. Criminal supervision orders made under section 7(7)(b) of the Children and Young Persons Act 1969 and those made under section 21(2) of the Children and Young Persons Act 1969 upon discharge of a criminal care order made under section 7(7) (a) of that Act will continue until terminated by existing arrangements under the Children and Young Persons Act 1969.

Place of Safety Orders

6.45. A place of safety order made under any of the provisions listed in paragraph 27(2) of Schedule 14 will continue to have effect as if the Children Act had not been passed. In addition, any enactments repealed by the Children Act shall continue to have effect so far as is necessary for carrying out the place of safety order as if the Children Act had not been passed.

6.46. The effect of this is that place of safety orders and detention under section 28 of the Children and Young Persons Act 1969 will continue unaffected by the Children Act until the expiry date which was decided upon by the court when the order was made and in accordance with the provisions of section 28 as to detention.

6.47. Any interim order made under section 23(5) of the Children and Young Persons Act 1963 or section 28(6) of the Children and Young Persons Act 1969 will, in the same way, continue to have effect as if the Children Act had not been passed. However, the provision that other repealed enactments will continue in force does not apply.

Foster Children (Private Children's Homes)

6.48. A private children's home, that is one in which more than three children are accommodated, where those children are not siblings and the person running the home has not been exempted from the usual fostering limit by the local authority, has three months from the date of commencement of the Act to put in an application for registration in accordance with the Children's Homes Regulations. (Such children come within the meaning of a 'foster child' in the Foster Children Act 1980). Provided an application is made no offence will be committed under section 63(10) unless the application has been refused, the appeal period has expired, or the appeal has been determined.

6.49. Until then the child shall continue to be treated as a privately fostered child and the private fostering guidance and regulations will apply. Where it is intended to seek exemption from the 'usual fostering limit' paragraph 32 of schedule 14 implicitly allows a private foster parent three months from the date of commencement of the Act to seek that exemption. Local authorities should, however, be encouraging applications for exemption to be made immediately so that exemptions, where appropriate, may be granted on 14 October 1991 or as soon after as is practicable.

Foster Parents: Limits on Numbers of Foster Children

6.50. Paragraph 2 of Schedule 7 to the Act prohibits foster parents approved by local authorities and voluntary organisations and those persons who are privately fostering from fostering more than three children ("the usual fostering limit") unless they have been exempted from this limit by the local authority.

6.51. *The "usual fostering limit" will come into force on 14 October 1991.* Therefore, local authorities and voluntary organisations should be considering the need for exemptions or new placements as they consider appropriate in time for 14 October alongside their work to ensure that the requirements of the Arrangements for Placement of Children (General) Regulations 1991 are met.They should also consider the need to exempt those privately fostering more than three children.

Nurseries and Childminders

6.52. These will have a year in which to register. Meanwhile the old 1948 Act will continue to apply, unless registration is granted earlier in which case the new law will apply from that date.

Children in Health Authority, Local Education Authority Accommodation, or in Residential Care Homes, Nursing Homes or Mental Nursing Homes

6.53. The relevant authority or person carrying on the home has three months from the date of commencement of the Act to notify the local authority of a child so accommodated for a consecutive period of at least three months unless it is known that the child will be accommodated for at least three months from 14 October 1991. Local authorities will need to inform these authorities and persons of this requirement.

Independent Schools

6.54. There are no transitional arrangements for those independent schools which provide accommodation for fifty or less children and which are required under section 63 to be registered as a children's home. Where a child is cared for and accommodated in a children's home which has not been registered as such the person carrying on the home shall be guilty of an offence unless he has a reasonable excuse (section 63(10)).

6.55. Section 87, which provides for the welfare of children accommodated in independent schools, other than those defined under the Act as a children's home or a residential care home, comes into effect as of 14 October 1991.

Local authorities will be expected to discharge their duties under this section as soon after 14 October as is reasonably practicable.

Criminal Care Orders

6.56. These are defined as orders made under section 7(7) (a) of the Children and Young Persons Act 1969 (alteration in treatment of young offenders etc) or section 15(I) of that Act when discharging a supervision order made under section 7(7)(b).

6.57. Where one of these orders is in force immediately before 14 October 1991, it continues to have effect for 6 months beginning on 14 October 1991 unless brought to an end earlier by a relevant provision of the 1969 Act or the Child Care Act 1980 which is preserved for as long as the order exists.

6.58. A criminal care order will be discharged if the court makes a residence order, care order, supervision order or education supervision order on the application of an appropriate person, ie the local authority, a local education authority or in the case of a residence order, anyone with the leave of the court. In addition the local authority can apply for a criminal supervision order with a residence requirement for a maximum period of six months. This short term removal from home requirement intended for the persistent offender, will provide the local authority with a limited opportunity to work with the child and the family.

6.59. Local authorities should carefully examine all existing criminal care orders and consider what action should be taken before or immediately following implementation of the Act. It should be borne in mind that an access order under section 12(C) of the 1980 Child Care Act will cease to have effect when the criminal care order is discharged by the making of a supervision order with a residence requirement. If the local authority wish to maintain a restricted contact regime and can satisfy the statutory threshold criteria they should consider applying for a care order instead.

CHAPTER 7 THE CRIMINAL JUSTICE ACT 1991

INTRODUCTION

7.1. The Criminal Justice Act 1991 contains a number of important provisions relating to young offenders which will have implications for local authorities in the way they exercise their responsibilities under the Children Act 1989. Detailed guidance about the 1991 Act, the main provisions of which are likely to be brought into force in October 1992, will be issued in due course. However, the following paragraphs highlight a number of important features of the Act which have implications for the way in which local authorities exercise their responsibilities towards children under the 1989 Act or which local authorities and other relevant agencies will need to take into account in planning and developing services.

CHILDREN'S EVIDENCE

7.2. Sections 52 to 55 make important changes to the law on the giving of evidence by children. These will be of particular relevance to children involved in cases of alleged sexual or physical assault. The changes cover the competence of children as witnesses; notices of transfer of certain cases involving children; the video recording of testimony from child witnesses, and the cross-examination of alleged child victims.

THE YOUTH COURT

7.3. With the introduction of family proceedings courts, the remit of the juvenile court will be confined to criminal matters. Under the Criminal Justice Act 1991 the juvenile court will be renamed the youth court (section 70) and its remit will be extended to include 17 year-olds who, for most purposes, will be treated as young persons rather than adults (section 68). Young people aged 17 will, however, continue to be treated as adults for pre-trial purposes.

DETENTION OF ARRESTED AND DETAINED JUVENILES AT A POLICE STATION

7.4. Arising from recent High Court Judgements about the interpretation of section 38(6) of the Police and Criminal Evidence Act 1984, the opportunity has been taken in section 59 of the 1991 Act to clarify the limited circumstances in which an arrested and detained juvenile might not otherwise be moved to local authority accommodation while awaiting appearance in court. The revised arrangements require such a juvenile to be moved to local authority accommodation unless the custody officer certifies either it is impracticable to do so, or, in the case of an arrested juvenile aged 15 or more, that no secure accommodation is available and that keeping him in other local authority accommodation would not be adequate to protect the public from serious harm (as defined in the Act) from him. The intention underlying the amended wording of section 38(6) is to ensure that, apart from cases where the juvenile is aged 15 years or over and protection of the public is an issue, how an arrested juvenile is to be accommodated by a local authority is not a relevant matter to be considered by the custody officer in determining whether or not it is practicable to move that juvenile to local authority accommodation. Guidance has already been provided in Chapter 6 of Volume 1 (Court Orders) in this series of Regulations and Guidance on the need for local authorities to review their present services and facilities to ensure compliance with their new duties under paragraph 7 of Schedule 2 of the 1989 Act (prevention of juvenile offending; reduce need to bring criminal proceedings). This review should also address services for arrested and detained juveniles.

JUVENILE REMANDS

7.5. Provision is made for the eventual abolition of the practice of remanding 15 and 16 year old males to prison department establishments (sections 60–62). This will be a two-stage process. Under *interim arrangements*, which are expected to come into force in October 1992, the option of a penal remand will remain available to the court in defined circumstances. The court will have a new power, after consultation with the local authority, to require any person remanded to local authority accommodation to comply with such conditions as it could impose under section 3(6) of the Bail Act 1976 if he were then granted bail. Again subject to consultation with the local authority, the court may impose requirements on that authority to secure compliance with any such conditions the court may have imposed on the child.

7.6. In the *longer term*, once there is general agreement that adequate alternative arrangements exist, juvenile penal remands will be abolished. Courts will then have a new power to direct that certain remanded juveniles must be placed in local authority secure accommodation. Local authorities will be placed under a duty to ensure that adequate secure accommodation exists for such purposes. The Secretary of State has Regulation-making power to specify how local authorities should cooperate to ensure such accommodation is provided. It is important that local authorities make an early start in planning for these changes in close consultation with other local authorities within their geographical area and with voluntary and other statutory agencies involved in the juvenile justice system.

PARENTAL RESPONSIBILITY

7.7. The Act creates a clear distinction between the measures available to the court for the 10–15 year old age group and for those aged 16–17 years old. For the younger age group a number of measures are designed to reinforce parental responsibility for the offender. Section 56 requires attendance at court of a parent or guardian during all stages of the proceedings involving their children aged under 16, unless it is unreasonable to require such attendance. Where a local authority has parental responsibility for the child the requirement to attend court falls on that authority.

7.8. Section 57 deals with the responsibility of a parent or guardian for financial penalties imposed on a child or young person. The section requires the means of the parents etc to be taken into consideration when they are being asked to pay financial penalties. For offenders aged 16–17, the present duty of the court to make an order requiring parents etc to pay financial penalties is replaced by a power to make such an order. Local authorities will be under a new duty to pay financial penalties imposed on offenders aged under 18 for whom they have parental responsibility.

SENTENCING POWERS OF THE COURT

7.9. The Act introduces a number of important further changes to the court process and the disposals available to the court. These include the requirement to obtain a pre-sentence report (from a probation officer or local authority social worker) when a custodial sentence is being considered; modifications to the criteria for custody; the relevance of previous convictions; the introduction of unit fines; the abolition of the custodial sentence for 14 year old males; the availability of the probation order for 16 year olds; the extension of supervision orders to 17 year olds; the increase in the maximum length of a community service order for 16 year olds to 240 hours; the introduction of a new combination order for those aged over 16; the introduction of curfew orders, and the possibility of electronic monitoring, for those aged 16 and over. As noted above, further guidance will be issued on all these provisions.

7.10. Local authorities should bear in mind that the introduction of the youth court will require careful local planning by all agencies in the juvenile justice system. In particular, the restructuring of community penalties and the availability of supervision orders, probation orders and combination orders for 16 and 17 year olds will require close consultation and cooperation between social services departments and the probation service. Social services departments may find it helpful to contact local probation departments at an early stage to discuss the development of a joint strategy for providing a comprehensive service to the courts for this client group and to explore the possibility of participating in joint training activities.

STATUTORY INSTRUMENTS

1991 No. 2051

CHILDREN AND YOUNG PERSONS

The Guardians Ad Litem and Reporting Officers (Panels) Regulations 1991

Made - - - -	*10th September 1991*
Laid before Parliament	*17th September 1991*
Coming into force	*14th October 1991*

The Secretary of State in exercise of the powers conferred by sections 41(7) and (9) and 104(4) of the Children Act 1989(**a**) and section 65A(1) and (2) of the Adoption Act 1976(**b**) and of all other powers enabling him in that behalf hereby makes the following Regulations:

Citation, commencement and interpretation

1.—(1) These Regulations may be cited as the Guardians Ad Litem and Reporting Officers (Panels) Regulations 1991 and shall come into force on 14th October 1991.

(2) In these Regulations, unless the context otherwise requires–

"complaints board" means a board established under regulation 3(a) of these Regulations;

"panel" means a panel established under regulation 2(1) of these Regulations;

"panel committee" means a committee established under regulation 3(b) of these Regulations;

"relevant proceedings" means specified proceedings as defined in section 41(6) of the Children Act 1989(**c**) or proceedings on an application for any order referred to in section 65 of the Adoption Act 1976.

Panels of guardians ad litem and reporting officers

2.—(1) Each local authority shall establish a panel of persons in accordance with regulation 4 of these Regulations in respect of their area.

(2) Guardians ad litem and reporting officers appointed under section 41 of the Children Act 1989 for the purposes of relevant proceedings or under rules made under Section 65 of the Adoption Act 1976 must be selected from the panel established in respect of the local authority's area in which the court is situated (unless selected from another local authority's panel established under these Regulations).

(3) Each local authority shall ensure that so far as possible the number of persons appointed to the panel established in respect of their area is sufficient to provide guardians ad litem and reporting officers for all relevant proceedings in which guardians ad litem and reporting officers may be appointed and which may be heard in their area.

(**a**) 1989 c.41.
(**b**) 1976 c.36. Section 65A was inserted by paragraph 29 of Schedule 10 to the Children Act 1989.
(**c**) *See* rule 4.2(2) of the Family Proceedings Rules 1991 (S.I. 1991/1247) and rule 2(2) of the Family Proceedings Courts (Children Act 1989) Rules 1991 (S.I. 1991/1395).

Complaints boards and panel committees

3. For the purpose of assisting them with matters concening the membership of panels, the administration and procedures of panels and the monitoring of the work of guardians ad litem and reporting officers in relevant proceedings, each local authority shall establish–

(a) a board ("complaints board") in accordance with Schedule 1 to these Regulations, which shall have the functions conferred on them by regulations 5 and 6 of these Regulations;

(b) a committee ("panel committee") in accordance with Schedule 2 to these Regulations, which shall have the functions conferred on it by regulations 8 and 10(1)(a) of these Regulations.

Appointments to panels

4.—(1) The local authority in respect of whose area the panel is established shall appoint persons to be members of the panel.

(2) The local authority shall decide whether the qualifications and experience of any person who they propose to appoint to the panel are suitable for the purposes of that person's appointment as a guardian ad litem or a reporting officer who they propose to appoint to the panel.

(3) The local authority shall in respect of any person whom they propose to appoint to the panel–

(a) interview each such person,

(b) consult the panel committee, and

(c) obtain the names of at least two persons who can provide a reference in writing for the persons whom they propose to appoint and take up those references.

(4) The local authority shall notify in writing any person who is appointed to a panel of the appointment which shall, subject to regulation 5 of these Regulations, be for such period not exceeding three years at any one time as the local authority shall specify on making the appointment.

(5) Each local authority shall maintain a record of those persons whom they have appointed to be members of the panel established in respect of their area.

(6) Every local authority shall have regard to the number of children in their area who may become the subject of specified proceedings and the different racial groups to which they belong, in making appointments under this regulation.

Termination of panel membership

5.—(1) The local authority may terminate a person's membership of the panel at any time where they consider that he is unable or unfit to carry out the functions of a guardian ad litem or a reporting officer.

(2) Before terminating a person's membership of the panel the local authority shall–

(a) notify him in writing of the reasons why it is proposed that his membership of the panel should be terminated;

(b) give him an opportunity of making representations to the local authority.

(3) Where the local authority, having considered any representations made under paragraph (2)(b) of this regulation, still propose to terminate a person's membership, they shall refer the matter to a complaints board.

(4) The complaints board shall make a recommendation to the authority after taking account of any representations of the person whose membership the local authority proposed to terminate.

(5) The local authority shall consider the recommendation of the complaints board, as to termination of a person's membership and decide whether or not to terminate membership and give notice to that person in writing of their decision together with their reasons for the decision.

Complaints about the operation of panels and members of the panels

6.—(1) For the purpose of monitoring the administration and procedures of the panel and the work of guardians ad litem and reporting officers in relevant proceedings each local authority shall establish a procedure for considering complaints about the operation of the panel in respect of their area, and about any member of that panel including refusal to reappoint a person to be a panel member.

(2) The local authority shall investigate any such complaint and if they cannot resolve it to the satisfaction of the person making it they shall refer it to the complaints board to make a recommendation to the authority about it in writing.

(3) Any person in respect of whom a complaint is made shall be notified by the local authority in writing of the complaint and they shall give him an opportunity of making representations to them and if the matter is referred to the complaints board they shall provide him with an opportunity to make representations to the complaints board.

(4) The local authority shall only make a decision on a complaint referred to the complaints board having taken into account the recommendation of the complaints board and they shall notify the person who made the complaint and any person in respect of whom the complaint was made in writing of their decision.

Administration of the panel

7.—(1) Each local authority shall appoint a person with such qualifications and experience as they consider appropriate to assist them with the administration of the panel in respect of their area and that person shall not participate in the local authority social services functions in respect of services for children and their families (other than the administration of the panel or an inspection unit established under the Secretary of State's directions under section 7A of the Local Authority Social Services Act 1970(**a**)).

(2) Each local authority shall ensure that records are kept in relation to the operation of the panel which shall include–

- (a) the name of each child in respect of whom a guardian ad litem or reporting officer is selected from the panel;
- (b) a description of the relevant proceedings in respect of which the selection is made;
- (c) the name and level of the court (whether High Court, county court or family proceedings court);
- (d) the name of any person selected from the panel and whether he has been appointed in specified proceedings or in proceedings under the Adoption Act 1976 as a guardian ad litem, or in proceedings under the Adoption Act 1976 as a reporting officer;
- (e) the date of each appointment, the date on which work started in respect of that appointment and the date on which it finished;
- (f) details of fees, expenses and allowances in each case in which there has been such an appointment;
- (g) the result of the proceedings in each case in which there has been such an appointment.

Panel committee functions

8. The local authority shall make arrangements for the panel committee to assist with liaison between the local authority in their administration of the panel and the courts in the local authority's area and to advise on–

- (a) the standards of practice of guardians ad litem and reporting officers in relevant proceedings in their area;
- (b) the appointment and reappointment of guardians ad litem and reporting officers to the panel, termination of their appointment and review of their work;
- (c) the training of guardians ad litem and reporting officers; and

(**a**) 1970 c.42. Section 7A was inserted by section 50 of the National Health Service and Community Care Act 1990 (c.19). The relevant direction establishing inspection units was issued with local authority circular LAC(90)13.

(d) matters arising from complaints concerning guardians ad litem, reporting officers and the administration of the panel (but not the investigation of particular complaints).

Expenses, fees and allowances of members of panels

9.—(1) Each local authority shall defray the reasonable expenses incurred in respect of relevant proceedings by members of the panel established in respect of their area and pay fees and allowances for members of such panels in respect of relevant proceedings.

(2) No expenses, fees and allowances referred to in paragraph (1) of this regulation shall be defrayed or paid by local authorities by virtue of paragraph (1) in respect of a member of a panel who is employed under a contract of service by a local authority or probation committee for thirty hours or more a week.

Monitoring the work of guardians ad litem and reporting officers

10.—(1) For the purposes of monitoring the work of guardians ad litem and reporting officers each local authority which has established a panel in respect of their area shall–

(a) obtain the views of the panel committee on the work of each member of the panel who has been appointed a guardian ad litem or reporting officer, and

(b) review the work of each such member of the panel

at least once during the first year of an appointment to the panel.

(2) The results of each review shall be recorded by the local authority in writing and they shall send a copy of the results to the member of the panel to whom they relate.

Training

11. The local authority shall, having regard to the cases in which members of the panel have been or may be appointed as a guardian ad litem or reporting officer, identify any training needs which members of the panel may have and make reasonable provision for such training.

Revocation of the Guardian Ad Litem and Reporting Officers (Panels) Regulations 1983 and Amendment Regulations 1986

12. The Guardians Ad Litem and Reporting Officers (Panels) Regulations 1983(**a**) and the Guardians Ad Litem and Reporting Officers (Panels) (Amendment) Regulations 1986(**b**) are hereby revoked.

Signed by authority of the Secretary of State for Health.

Virginia Bottomley
Minister of State,
Department of Health

10th September 1991

(**a**) S.I. 1983/1908.
(**b**) S.I. 1986/3.

SCHEDULE 1

Regulation 3(a)

Complaints Board

The complaints board shall consist of three persons, –

(a) one of whom shall be a person who is neither an officer nor a member of a local authority;

(b) another of whom shall be a person who is involved in the functions in respect of services for children and their families of a local authority which has not established the panel;

(c) another of whom shall be a justices' clerk of a magistrates' court in the local authority's area.

SCHEDULE 2

Regulation 3(b)

Panel Committee

1. The panel committee shall consist of at least one of the following –

(a) a representative of the local authority;

(b) a justices' clerk of a magistrates' court in the local authority's area;

(c) a person who has relevant experience of child care who is neither an officer nor a member of a local authority;

(d) a representative of the panel established under regulation 2(1) of these Regulations.

2. The panel committee shall not be chaired by a representative of the local authority.

3. The membership of the panel committee shall not consist of a majority of representatives of the local authority.

4. Appointments to the panel committee shall be for such period not exceeding three years at any one time as the authority shall specify on making the appointment.

EXPLANATORY NOTE

(This note does not form part of the Regulations)

These Regulations make provision for the establishment of panels of guardians ad litem and reporting officers by local authorities (regulation 2); complaints boards and panel committees (regulation 3); appointments to panels (regulation 4); termination of panel membership (regulation 5); complaints about the operation of the panels and members of the panels (regulation 6); administration of panels (regulation 7); panel committee functions (regulation 8); expenses, fees and allowances of panel members (regulation 9); monitoring the work of guardians ad litem and reporting officers (regulation 10); training (regulation 11) and revocation of the Guardian Ad Litem and Reporting Officers (Panels) Regulations 1983 and the Amendment Regulations 1986 which these 1991 Regulations replace (regulation 12);

The principal changes from the arrangements in respect of panels under the 1983 Regulations are that a complaints board and panel committee are to be established to assist the authority in administration of the panel and the procedure for termination of appointments to the panel and administration of the panel is specified in greater detail in the Regulations.

£1.45 net

ISBN 0 11 015051 1

Printed in the United Kingdom for HMSO

879/WO 1779 C40 9/91 452/1 9385/3873/1753 134952

ANNEX B

COPY OF – THE FAMILY PROCEEDINGS COURTS (CHILDREN ACT) RULES 1991 (SI 1395), Pp 1–18 only

STATUTORY INSTRUMENTS

1991 No. 1395 (L.17)

MAGISTRATES' COURTS

The Family Proceedings Courts (Children Act 1989) Rules 1991

Made - - - -	*25th May 1991*
Laid before Parliament	*12th July 1991*
Coming into force -	*14th October 1991*

ARRANGEMENT OF RULES

PART I

Introductory

PART II

General

PART III

Miscellaneous

SCHEDULES

The Lord Chancellor, in exercise of the powers conferred on him by section 144 of the Magistrates' Courts Act 1980**(a)**, after consultation with the Rule Committee appointed under that section, hereby makes the following Rules:–

(a) 1980 c.43, as extended by sections 74 and 145 of that Act; by section 28 of the Justices of the Peace Act 1979 (c.55); and by sections 11(2), 32(2), 41(2), (5), (6)(i) and (10), 38(8)(b), 43(12), 44(9)(b), 48(12), 52(1) and (2), 93, 95(2), 97(1) and 102(4) of the Children Act 1989 (c.41).

PART I

INTRODUCTORY

Citation, commencement and interpretation

1.—(1) These Rules may be cited as the Family Proceedings Courts (Children Act 1989) Rules 1991 and shall come into force on 14th October 1991.

(2) Unless a contrary intention appears–

a section or schedule referred to means the section or schedule in the Act of 1989,

"application" means an application made under or by virtue of the Act of 1989 or under these Rules, and "applicant" shall be construed accordingly,

"business day" means any day other than–

(a) a Saturday, Sunday, Christmas Day or Good Friday; or

(b) a bank holiday, that is to say, a day which is, or is to be observed as, a bank holiday, or a holiday, under the Banking and Financial Dealings Act 1971**(a)**, in England and Wales,

"child"

(a) means, in relation to any relevant proceedings, subject to sub-paragraph (b), a person under the age of 18 with respect to whom the proceedings are brought, and

(b) where paragraph 16(1) of Schedule 1 applies, also includes a person who has reached the age of 18;

"contribution order" has the meaning assigned to it by paragraph 23(2) of Schedule 2,

"court" means a family proceedings court constituted in accordance with sections 66 and 67 of the Magistrates' Courts Act 1980 or, in respect of those proceedings prescribed in rule 2(5), a single justice who is a member of a family panel,

"directions appointment" means a hearing for directions under rule 14(2),

"emergency protection order" means an order under section 44,

"file" means deposit with the justices' clerk,

"form" means a form in Schedule 1 to these Rules with such variation as the circumstances of the particular case may require,

"guardian ad litem" means a guardian ad litem, appointed under section 41, of the child with respect to whom the proceedings are brought,

"justices' clerk" has the meaning assigned to it by section 70 of the Justices of the Peace Act 1979 and includes any person who performs a justices' clerk's functions by virtue of rule 32,

"leave" includes approval,

"note" includes a record made by mechanical means,

"parental responsibility" has the meaning assigned to it by section 3,

"parties" in relation to any relevant proceedings means the respondents specified for those proceedings in the third column of Schedule 2 to these Rules, and the applicant,

"recovery order" means an order under section 50,

"relevant proceedings" has the meaning assigned to it by section 93(3),

"section 8 order" has the meaning assigned to it by section 8(2),

"specified proceedings" has the meaning assigned to it by section 41(6) and rule 2(2),

"the 1981 rules" means the Magistrates' Courts Rules 1981**(b)**,

"the Act of 1989" means the Children Act 1989**(c)**,

"welfare officer" means a person who has been asked to prepare a welfare report under section 7.

(a) 1971 c.80.

(b) S.I. 1981/552, amended by 1982/245, 1983/523, 1984/1552, 1985/1695 and 1944, 1986/1332, 1988/2132, 1989/300 and 384, 1990/336, 1190 and 2260.

(c) 1989 c.41.

Matters prescribed for the purposes of the Act of 1989

2.—(1) The parties to proceedings in which directions are given under section 38(6), and any person named in such a direction, form the prescribed class for the purposes of section 38(8)(b) (application to vary directions made with interim care or interim supervision order).

(2) The following proceedings are specified for the purposes of section 41 in accordance with subsection (6)(i) thereof–

(a) proceedings under section 25;

(b) applications under section 33(7);

(c) proceedings under paragraph 19(1) of Schedule 2;

(d) applications under paragraph 6(3) of Schedule 3.

(3) The applicant for an order that has been made under section 43(1) and the persons referred to in section 43(11) may, in any circumstances, apply under section 43(12) for a child assessment order to be varied or discharged.

(4) The following persons form the prescribed class for the purposes of section 44(9)(b) (application to vary directions)–

(a) the parties to the application for the order in respect of which it is sought to vary the directions;

(b) the guardian ad litem;

(c) the local authority in whose area the child concerned is ordinarily resident;

(d) any person who is named in the directions.

(5) The following proceedings are prescribed for the purposes of section 93(2)(i) as being proceedings with respect to which a single justice may discharge the functions of a family proceedings court, that is to say, proceedings–

(a) where an ex parte application is made, under sections 10, 44(1), 48(9), 50(1), 75(1) or 102(1),

(b) subject to rule 28, under sections 11(3) or 38(1),

(c) under sections 4(3)(b), 7, 14, 34(3)(b), 37, 41, 44(9)(b) and (11)(b)(iii), 48(4), 91(15) or (17), or paragraph 11(4) of Schedule 14,

(d) in accordance with any Order made by the Lord Chancellor under Part I of Schedule 11, and

(e) in accordance with rules 3 to 8, 10 to 19, 21, 22, or 27.

PART II

GENERAL

Application for leave to commence proceedings

3.—(1) Where the leave of the court is required to bring any relevant proceedings, the person seeking leave shall file–

(a) a written request for leave setting out the reasons for the application; and

(b) a draft of the application for the making of which leave is sought in the appropriate form in Schedule 1 to these Rules or, where there is no such form, in writing, together with sufficient copies for one to be served on each respondent.

(2) On considering a request for leave filed under paragraph (1), the court shall–

(a) grant the request, whereupon the justices' clerk shall inform the person making the request of the decision, or

(b) direct that a date be fixed for a hearing of the request, whereupon the justices' clerk shall fix such a date and give such notice as the court directs to the person making the request and to such other persons as the court requires to be notified, of the date so fixed.

(3) Where leave is granted to bring any relevant proceedings, the application shall proceed in accordance with rule 4; but paragraph (1)(a) of that rule shall not apply.

Application

4.—(1) Subject to paragraph (4), an applicant shall–

(a) file the application in respect of each child in the appropriate form in Schedule 1 to these Rules or where there is no such form, in writing, together with sufficient copies for one to be served on each respondent, and

(b) serve a copy of the application, endorsed in accordance with paragraph (2)(b), on each respondent such minimum number of days prior to the date fixed under paragraph (2)(a) as is specified in relation to that application in column (ii) of Schedule 2 to these Rules.

(2) On receipt of the documents filed under paragraph (1)(a), the justices' clerk shall–

(a) fix the date, time and place for a hearing or a directions appointment, allowing sufficient time for the applicant to comply with paragraph (1)(b),

(b) endorse the date, time and place so fixed upon the copies of the application filed by the applicant, and

(c) return the copies to the applicant forthwith.

(3) The applicant shall, at the same time as complying with paragraph (1)(b), give written notice of the proceedings, and of the date, time and place of the hearing or appointment fixed under paragraph (2)(a) to the persons set out in relation to the relevant class of proceedings in column (iv) of Schedule 2 to these Rules.

(4) An application for–

(a) a prohibited steps order, or a specific issue order, under section 8,

(b) an emergency protection order,

(c) a warrant under section 48(9),

(d) a recovery order, or

(e) a warrant under section 102(1),

may, with leave of the justices' clerk, be made ex parte in which case the applicant shall–

(i) file with the justices' clerk or the court the application in respect of each child in the appropriate form in Schedule 1 to these Rules at the time when the application is made or as directed by the justices' clerk, and

(ii) in the case of an application for a prohibited steps order, or a specific issue order, under section 8 or an emergency protection order, and also in the case of an application for an order under section 75(1) where the application is ex parte, serve a copy of the application on each respondent within 48 hours after the making of the order.

(5) Where the court refuses to make an order on an ex parte application it may direct that the application be made inter partes.

(6) In the case of proceedings under Schedule 1, the application under paragraph (1) shall be accompanied by a statement setting out the financial details which the applicant believes to be relevant to the application and containing a declaration that it is true to the maker's best knowledge and belief, together with sufficient copies for one to be served on each respondent.

Withdrawal of application

5.—(1) An application may be withdrawn only with leave of the court.

(2) Subject to paragraph (3), a person seeking leave to withdraw an application shall file and serve on the parties a written request for leave setting out the reasons for the request.

(3) The request under paragraph (2) may be made orally to the court if the parties and, if appointed, the guardian ad litem or the welfare officer are present.

(4) Upon receipt of a written request under paragraph (2), the court shall–

(a) if–

(i) the parties consent in writing,

(ii) any guardian ad litem has had an opportunity to make representations, and

(iii) the court thinks fit,

grant the request; in which case the justices' clerk shall notify the parties, the guardian ad litem and the welfare officer of the granting of the request; or

(b) the justices' clerk shall fix a date for the hearing of the request and give at least 7 days' notice to the parties, the guardian ad litem and the welfare officer of the date fixed.

Transfer of proceedings

6.—(1) Where, in any relevant proceedings, the justices' clerk or the court receives a request in writing from a party that the proceedings be transferred to another family proceedings court or to a county court, the justices' clerk or court shall issue a certificate in the appropriate form in Schedule 1 to these Rules, granting or refusing the request in accordance with any Order made by the Lord Chancellor under Part I of Schedule 11.

(2) Where a request is granted under paragraph (1), the justices' clerk shall send a copy of the certificate–

(a) to the parties,

(b) to any guardian ad litem, and

(c) to the family proceedings court or to the county court to which the proceedings are to be transferred.

(3) Any consent given or refused by a justices' clerk in accordance with any Order made by the Lord Chancellor under Part I of Schedule 11 shall be recorded in writing by the justices' clerk at the time it is given or refused or as soon as practicable thereafter.

(4) Where a request to transfer proceedings to a county court is refused under paragraph (1), the person who made the request may apply in accordance with rule 4.6 of the Family Proceedings Rules 1991**(a)** for an order under any Order made by the Lord Chancellor under Part I of Schedule 11.

Parties

7.—(1) The respondents to relevant proceedings shall be those persons set out in the relevant entry in column (iii) of Schedule 2 to these Rules.

(2) In any relevant proceedings a person may file a request in writing that he or another person–

(a) be joined as a party, or

(b) cease to be a party.

(3) On considering a request under paragraph (2) the court shall, subject to paragraph (4)–

(a) grant it without a hearing or representations, save that this shall be done only in the case of a request under paragraph (2)(a), whereupon the justices' clerk shall inform the parties and the person making the request of that decision, or

(b) order that a date be fixed for the consideration of the request, whereupon the justices' clerk shall give notice of the date so fixed, together with a copy of the request–

(i) in the case of a request under paragraph (2)(a), to the applicant, and

(ii) in the case of a request under paragraph (2)(b), to the parties, or

(c) invite the parties or any of them to make written representations, within a specified period, as to whether the request should be granted; and upon the expiry of the period the court shall act in accordance with sub-paragraph (a) or (b).

(a) S.I. 1991/1247.

(4) Where a person with parental responsibility requests that he be joined under paragraph (2)(a), the court shall grant his request.

(5) In any relevant proceedings the court may direct–

(a) that a person who would not otherwise be a respondent under these Rules be joined as a party to the proceedings, or

(b) that a party to the proceedings cease to be a party.

Service

8.—(1) Where service of a document is required by these Rules (and not by a provision to which section 105(8) (service of notice or other document under the Act) applies) it may be effected–

(a) if the person to be served is not known by the person serving to be acting by solicitor–

(i) by delivering it to him personally, or

(ii) by delivering it at, or by sending it by first-class post to, his residence or his last known residence, or

(b) if the person to be served is known by the person serving to be acting by solicitor–

(i) by delivering the document at, or sending it by first-class post to, the solicitor's address for service,

(ii) where the solicitor's address for service includes a numbered box at a document exchange, by leaving the document at that document exchange or at a document exchange which transmits documents on every business day to that document exchange, or

(iii) by sending a legible copy of the document by facsimile transmission to the solicitor's office.

(2) In this rule, "first-class post" means first-class post which has been pre-paid or in respect of which pre-payment is not required.

(3) Where a child who is a party to any relevant proceedings is required by these Rules to serve a document, service shall be effected by–

(a) the solicitor acting for the child,

(b) where there is no such solicitor, the guardian ad litem, or

(c) where there is neither such a solicitor nor a guardian ad litem, the justices' clerk.

(4) Service of any document on a child shall, subject to any direction of the justices' clerk or the court, be effected by service on–

(a) the solicitor acting for the child,

(b) where there is no such solicitor, the guardian ad litem, or

(c) where there is neither such a solicitor nor a guardian ad litem, with leave of the justices' clerk or the court, the child.

(5) Where the justices' clerk or the court refuses leave under paragraph (4)(c), a direction shall be given under paragraph (8).

(6) A document shall, unless the contrary is proved, be deemed to have been served–

(a) in the case of service by first-class post, on the second business day after posting, and

(b) in the case of service in accordance with paragraph (1)(b)(ii), on the second business day after the day on which it is left at the document exchange.

(7) At or before the first directions appointment in, or hearing of, relevant proceedings, whichever occurs first, the applicant shall file a statement that service of–

(a) a copy of the application has been effected on each respondent, and

(b) notice of the proceedings has been effected under rule 4(3);

and the statement shall indicate–

(i) the manner, date, time and place of service, or

(ii) where service was effected by post, the date, time and place of posting.

(8) In any relevant proceedings, the justices' clerk or the court may direct that a requirement of these Rules to serve a document shall not apply or shall be effected in such manner as the justices' clerk or court directs.

Answer to application

9.—(1) Within 14 days of service of an application for a section 8 order, each respondent shall file and serve on the parties an answer to the application in the appropriate form in Schedule 1 to these Rules.

(2) Within 14 days of service of an application under Schedule 1, each respondent shall file and serve on the parties an answer to the application in the appropriate form in Schedule 1 to these Rules.

Appointment of guardian ad litem

10.—(1) As soon as practicable after the commencement of specified proceedings or the transfer of such proceedings to the court, the justices' clerk or the court shall appoint a guardian ad litem unless–

(a) such an appointment has already been made by the court which made the transfer and is subsisting, or

(b) the justices' clerk or the court considers that such an appointment is not necessary to safeguard the interests of the child.

(2) At any stage in specified proceedings a party may apply, without notice to the other parties unless the justices' clerk or the court otherwise directs, for the appointment of a guardian ad litem.

(3) The justices' clerk or the court shall grant an application under paragraph (2) unless it is considered that such an appointment is not necessary to safeguard the interests of the child, in which case reasons shall be given; and a note of such reasons shall be taken by the justices' clerk.

(4) At any stage in specified proceedings the justices' clerk or the court may appoint a guardian ad litem even though no application is made for such an appointment.

(5) The justices' clerk shall, as soon as practicable, notify the parties and any welfare officer of an appointment under this rule or, as the case may be, of a decision not to make such an appointment.

(6) Upon the appointment of a guardian ad litem the justices' clerk shall, as soon as practicable, notify him of the appointment and serve on him copies of the application and of documents filed under rule 17(1).

(7) A guardian ad litem appointed from a panel established by regulations made under section 41(7) shall not–

(a) be a member, officer or servant of a local authority which, or an authorised person (within the meaning of section 31(9)) who, is a party to the proceedings unless he is employed by such an authority solely as a member of a panel of guardians ad litem and reporting officers;

(b) be, or have been, a member, officer or servant of a local authority or voluntary organisation (within the meaning of section 105(1)) who has been directly concerned in that capacity in arrangements relating to the care, accommodation or welfare of the child during the five years prior to the commencement of the proceedings;

(c) be a serving probation officer (except that a probation officer who has not in that capacity been previously concerned with the child or his family and who is employed part-time may, when not engaged in his duties as a probation officer, act as a guardian ad litem).

(8) When appointing a guardian ad litem, the justices' clerk or the court shall consider the appointment of anyone who has previously acted as guardian ad litem of the same child.

(9) The appointment of a guardian ad litem under this rule shall continue for such time as is specified in the appointment or until terminated by the court.

(10) When terminating an appointment in accordance with paragraph (9), the court shall give reasons in writing for so doing, a note of which shall be taken by the justices' clerk.

(11) Where the justices' clerk or the court appoints a guardian ad litem in accordance with this rule or refuses to make such an appointment, the justices' clerk shall record the appointment or refusal in the appropriate form in Schedule 1 to these Rules.

Powers and duties of guardian ad litem

11.—(1) In carrying out his duty under section 41(2), the guardian ad litem shall have regard to the principle set out in section 1(2) and the matters set out in section 1(3)(a) to (f) as if for the word "court" in that section there were substituted the words "guardian ad litem".

(2) The guardian ad litem shall–

(a) appoint a solicitor to represent the child, unless such a solicitor has already been appointed, and

(b) give such advice to the child as is appropriate having regard to his understanding and, subject to rule 12(1)(a), instruct the solicitor representing the child on all matters relevant to the interests of the child, including possibilities for appeal, arising in the course of the proceedings.

(3) Where it appears to the guardian ad litem that the child–

(a) is instructing his solicitor direct, or

(b) intends to, and is capable of, conducting the proceedings on his own behalf,

he shall so inform the court through the justices' clerk and thereafter–

(i) shall perform all of his duties set out in this rule, other than duties under paragraph (2)(a) and such other duties as the justices' clerk or the court may direct,

(ii) shall take such part in the proceedings as the justices' clerk or the court may direct, and

(iii) may, with leave of the justices' clerk or the court, have legal representation in his conduct of those duties.

(4) The guardian ad litem shall, unless excused by the justices' clerk or the court, attend all directions appointments in, and hearings of, the proceedings and shall advise the justices' clerk or the court on the following matters–

(a) whether the child is of sufficient understanding for any purpose including the child's refusal to submit to a medical or psychiatric examination or other assessment that the court has power to require, direct or order;

(b) the wishes of the child in respect of any matter relevant to the proceedings, including his attendance at court;

(c) the appropriate forum for the proceedings;

(d) the appropriate timing of the proceedings or any part of them;

(e) the options available to it in respect of the child and the suitability of each such option including what order should be made in determining the application;

(f) any other matter concerning which the justices' clerk or the court seeks his advice or concerning which he considers that the justices' clerk or the court should be informed.

(5) The advice given under paragraph (4) may, subject to any order of the court, be given orally or in writing; and if the advice be given orally, a note of it shall be taken by the justices' clerk or the court.

(6) The guardian ad litem shall, where practicable, notify any person whose joinder as a party to those proceedings would be likely, in the guardian ad litem's opinion, to safeguard the interests of the child, of that person's right to apply to be joined under rule 7(2) and shall inform the justices' clerk or the court–

(a) of any such notification given,

(b) of anyone whom he attempted to notify under this paragraph but was unable to contact, and
(c) of anyone whom he believes may wish to be joined to the proceedings.

(7) The guardian ad litem shall, unless the justices' clerk or the court otherwise directs, not less than 7 days before the date fixed for the final hearing of the proceedings, file a written report advising on the interests of the child; and the justices' clerk shall, as soon as practicable, serve a copy of the report on the parties.

(8) The guardian ad litem shall serve and accept service of documents on behalf of the child in accordance with rule 8(3)(b) and (4)(b) and, where the child has not himself been served, and has sufficient understanding, advise the child of the contents of any documents so served.

(9) The guardian ad litem shall make such investigations as may be necessary for him to carry out his duties and shall, in particular–

(a) contact or seek to interview such persons as he thinks appropriate or as the court directs,
(b) if he inspects records of the kinds referred to in section 42, bring to the attention of the court, through the justices' clerk, and such other persons as the justices' clerk or the court may direct, all such records and documents which may, in his opinion, assist in the proper determination of the proceedings, and
(c) obtain such professional assistance as is available to him which he thinks appropriate or which the justices' clerk or the court directs him to obtain.

(10) In addition to his duties under other paragraphs of this rule, the guardian ad litem shall provide to the justices' clerk and the court such other assistance as may be required.

(11) A party may question the guardian ad litem about oral or written advice tendered by him to the justices' clerk or the court under this rule.

Solicitor for child

12.—(1) A solicitor appointed under section 41(3) or in accordance with rule 11(2)(a) shall represent the child–

(a) in accordance with instructions received from the guardian ad litem (unless the solicitor considers, having taken into account the views of the guardian ad litem and any direction of the court under rule 11(3), that the child wishes to give instructions which conflict with those of the guardian ad litem and that he is able, having regard to his understanding, to give such instructions on his own behalf in which case he shall conduct the proceedings in accordance with instructions received from the child), or
(b) where no guardian ad litem has been appointed for the child and the condition in section 41(4)(b) is satisfied, in accordance with instructions received from the child, or
(c) in default of instructions under (a) or (b), in furtherance of the best interests of the child.

(2) A solicitor appointed under section 41(3) or in accordance with rule 11(2)(a) shall serve and accept service of documents on behalf of the child in accordance with rule 8(3)(a) and (4)(a) and, where the child has not himself been served and has sufficient understanding, advise the child of the contents of any document so served.

(3) Where the child wishes an appointment of a solicitor under section 41(3) or in accordance with rule 11(2)(a) to be terminated, he may apply to the court for an order terminating the appointment; and the solicitor and the guardian ad litem shall be given an opportunity to make representations.

(4) Where the guardian ad litem wishes an appointment of a solicitor under section 41(3) to be terminated, he may apply to the court for an order terminating the appointment; and the solicitor and, if he is of sufficient understanding, the child, shall be given an opportunity to make representations.

(5) When terminating an appointment in accordance with paragraph (3) or (4), the court shall give reasons for so doing, a note of which shall be taken by the justices' clerk.

(6) Where the justices' clerk or the court appoints a solicitor under section 41(3) or refuses to make such an appointment, the justices' clerk shall record the appointment or refusal in the appropriate form in Schedule 1 to these Rules and serve a copy on the parties and, where he is appointed, on the solicitor.

Welfare officer

13.—(1) The welfare officer shall, unless excused by the court or the justices' clerk, attend a hearing if the justices' clerk gives him notice that his report will be given or considered at that hearing; and any party may question the welfare officer about his report at such a hearing.

(2) A welfare officer shall file a copy of any written report at or by such time as the justices' clerk or the court directs or, in the absence of a direction, at least 5 days before a hearing of which he is given notice under paragraph (1); and the justices' clerk shall, as soon as practicable, serve a copy of the report on the parties and any guardian ad litem.

Directions

14.—(1) In this rule, "party" includes the guardian ad litem and, where a request or direction concerns a report under section 7, the welfare officer.

(2) In any relevant proceedings the justices' clerk or the court may, subject to paragraph (5), give, vary or revoke directions for the conduct of the proceedings, including–

- (a) the timetable for the proceedings;
- (b) varying the time within which or by which an act is required, by these Rules, to be done;
- (c) the attendance of the child;
- (d) the appointment of a guardian ad litem whether under section 41 or otherwise, or of a solicitor under section 41(3);
- (e) the service of documents;
- (f) the submission of evidence including experts' reports;
- (g) the preparation of welfare reports under section 7;
- (h) the transfer of the proceedings to another court in accordance with any Order made by the Lord Chancellor under Part I of Schedule 11;
- (i) consolidation with other proceedings;

and the justices' clerk shall, on receipt of an application, or where proceedings have been transferred to his court, consider whether such directions need to be given.

(3) Where the justices' clerk or a single justice who is holding a directions appointment considers, for whatever reason, that it is inappropriate to give a direction on a particular matter, he shall refer the matter to the court which may give any appropriate direction.

(4) Where a direction is given under paragraph (2)(h), a certificate shall be issued in the appropriate form in Schedule 1 to these Rules and the justices' clerk shall follow the procedure set out in rule 6(2).

(5) Directions under paragraph (2) may be given, varied or revoked either–

- (a) of the justices' clerk or the court's own motion having given the parties notice of the intention to do so and an opportunity to attend and be heard or to make written representations,
- (b) on the written request of a party specifying the direction which is sought, filed and served on the other parties, or
- (c) on the written request of a party specifying the direction which is sought, to which the other parties consent and which they or their representatives have signed.

(6) In an urgent case, the request under paragraph (5)(b) may, with the leave of the justices' clerk or the court, be made–

(a) orally,

(b) without notice to the parties, or

(c) both as in sub-paragraph (a) and as in sub-paragraph (b).

(7) On receipt of a request under paragraph (5)(b) the justices' clerk shall fix a date for the hearing of the request and give not less than 2 days' notice to the parties of the date so fixed.

(8) On considering a request under paragraph (5)(c) the justices' clerk or the court shall either–

(a) grant the request, whereupon the justices' clerk shall inform the parties of the decision, or

(b) direct that a date be fixed for the hearing of the request, whereupon the justices' clerk shall fix such a date and give not less than 2 days' notice to the parties of the date so fixed.

(9) Subject to rule 28, a party may request, in accordance with paragraph 5(b) or (c), that an order be made under section 11(3) or, if he is entitled to apply for such an order, under section 38(1), and paragraphs (6), (7) and (8) shall apply accordingly.

(10) Where, in any relevant proceedings, the court has power to make an order of its own motion, the power to give directions under paragraph (2) shall apply.

(11) Directions of the justices' clerk or a court which are still in force immediately prior to the transfer of relevant proceedings to another court shall continue to apply following the transfer, subject to any changes of terminology which are required to apply those directions to the court to which the proceedings are transferred, unless varied or discharged by directions under paragraph (2).

(12) The justices' clerk or the court shall take a note of the giving, variation or revocation of a direction under this rule and serve, as soon as practicable, a copy of the note on any party who was not present at the giving, variation or revocation.

Timing of proceedings

15.—(1) Any period of time fixed by these Rules, or by any order or direction, for doing any act shall be reckoned in accordance with this rule.

(2) Where the period, being a period of 7 days or less, would include a day which is not a business day, that day shall be excluded.

(3) Where the time fixed for filing a document with the justices' clerk expires on a day on which the justices' clerk's office is closed, and for that reason the document cannot be filed on that day, the document shall be filed in time if it is filed on the next day on which the justices' clerk's office is open.

(4) Where these Rules provide a period of time within which or by which a certain act is to be performed in the course of relevant proceedings, that period may not be extended otherwise than by a direction of the justices' clerk or the court under rule 14.

(5) At the–

(a) transfer to a court of relevant proceedings,

(b) postponement or adjournment of any hearing or directions appointment in the course of relevant proceedings, or

(c) conclusion of any such hearing or directions appointment other than one at which the proceedings are determined, or so soon thereafter as is practicable,

the justices' clerk or the court shall–

(i) fix a date upon which the proceedings shall come before the justices' clerk or the court again for such purposes as the justices' clerk or the court directs, which date shall, where paragraph (a) applies, be as soon as possible after the transfer, and

(ii) give notice to the parties and to the guardian ad litem or the welfare officer of the date so fixed.

Attendance at directions appointment and hearing

16.—(1) Subject to paragraph (2), a party shall attend a directions appointment of which he has been given notice in accordance with rule 14(5) unless the justices' clerk or the court otherwise directs.

(2) Relevant proceedings shall take place in the absence of any party including the child if–

(a) the court considers it in the interests of the child, having regard to the matters to be discussed or the evidence likely to be given, and

(b) the party is represented by a guardian ad litem or solicitor;

and when considering the interests of the child under sub-paragraph (a) the court shall give the guardian ad litem, solicitor for the child and, if he is of sufficient understanding, the child, an opportunity to make representations.

(3) Subject to paragraph (4) below, where at the time and place appointed for a hearing or directions appointment the applicant appears but one or more of the respondents do not, the justices' clerk or the court may proceed with the hearing or appointment.

(4) The court shall not begin to hear an application in the absence of a respondent unless–

(a) it is proved to the satisfaction of the court that he received reasonable notice of the date of the hearing; or

(b) the court is satisfied that the circumstances of the case justify proceeding with the hearing.

(5) Where, at the time and place appointed for a hearing or directions appointment, one or more respondents appear but the applicant does not, the court may refuse the application or, if sufficient evidence has previously been received, proceed in the absence of the applicant.

(6) Where at the time and place appointed for a hearing or directions appointment neither the applicant nor any respondent appears, the court may refuse the application.

(7) If the court considers it expedient in the interests of the child, it shall hear any relevant proceedings in private when only the officers of the court, the parties, their legal representatives and such other persons as specified by the court may attend.

Documentary Evidence

17.—(1) Subject to paragraphs (4) and (5), in any relevant proceedings a party shall file and serve on the parties, any welfare officer and any guardian ad litem of whose appointment he has been given notice under rule 10(5)–

(a) written statements of the substance of the oral evidence which the party intends to adduce at a hearing of, or a directions appointment in, those proceedings, which shall–

(i) be dated,

(ii) be signed by the person making the statement, and

(iii) contain a declaration that the maker of the statement believes it to be true and understands that it may be placed before the court, and

(b) copies of any documents, including, subject to rule 18(3), experts' reports, upon which the party intends to rely, at a hearing of, or a directions appointment in, those proceedings,

at or by such time as the justices' clerk or the court directs or, in the absence of a direction, before the hearing or appointment.

(2) A party may, subject to any direction of the justices' clerk or the court about the timing of statements under this rule, file and serve on the parties a statement which is supplementary to a statement served under paragraph (1).

(3) At a hearing or directions appointment a party may not, without the leave of the justices' clerk, in the case of a directions appointment, or the court–

(a) adduce evidence, or

(b) seek to rely on a document,

in respect of which he has failed to comply with the requirements of paragraph (1).

(4) In proceedings for a section 8 order a party shall–

(a) neither file nor serve any document other than as required or authorised by these Rules, and

(b) in completing a form prescribed by these Rules, neither give information, nor make a statement, which is not required or authorised by that form,

without the leave of the justices' clerk or the court.

(5) In proceedigs for a section 8 order, no statement or copy may be filed under paragraph (1) until such time as the justices' clerk or the court directs.

Expert evidence – examination of child

18.—(1) No person may, without the leave of the justices' clerk or the court, cause the child to be medically or psychiatrically examined, or otherwise assessed, for the purpose of the preparation of expert evidence for use in the proceedings.

(2) An application for leave under paragraph (1) shall, unless the justices' clerk or the court otherwise directs, be served on all the parties to the proceedings and on the guardian ad litem.

(3) Where the leave of the justices' clerk or the court has not been given under paragraph (1), no evidence arising out of an examination or assessment to which that paragraph applies may be adduced without the leave of the court.

Amendment

19.—(1) Subject to rule 17(2), a document which has been filed or served in any relevant proceedings may not be amended without the leave of the justices' clerk or the court which shall, unless the justices' clerk or the court otherwise directs, be requested in writing.

(2) On considering a request for leave to amend a document the justices' clerk or the court shall either–

(a) grant the request, whereupon the justices' clerk shall inform the person making the request of that decision, or

(b) invite the parties or any of them to make representations, within a specified period, as to whether such an order should be made.

(3) A person amending a document shall file it with the justices' clerk and serve it on those persons on whom it was served prior to amendment; and the amendments shall be identified.

Oral Evidence

20. The justices' clerk or the court shall keep a note of the substance of the oral evidence given at a hearing of, or directions appointment in, relevant proceedings.

Hearing

21.—(1) Before the hearing, the justice or justices who will be dealing with the case shall read any documents which have been filed under rule 17 in respect of the hearing.

(2) The justices' clerk at a directions appointment, or the court at a hearing or directions appointment, may give directions as to the order of speeches and evidence.

(3) Subject to directions under paragraph (2), at a hearing of, or directions appointment in, relevant proceedings, the parties and the guardian ad litem shall adduce their evidence in the following order–

(a) the applicant,

(b) any party with parental responsibility for the child,

(c) other respondents,

(d) the guardian ad litem,

(e) the child if he is a party to the proceedings and there is no guardian ad litem.

(4) After the final hearing of relevant proceedings, the court shall make its decision as soon as is practicable.

(5) Before the court makes an order or refuses an application or request, the justices' clerk shall record in writing–

(a) the names of the justice or justices constituting the court by which the decision is made, and

(b) in consultation with the justice or justices, the reasons for the court's decision and any findings of fact.

(6) When making an order or when refusing an application, the court, or one of the justices constituting the court by which the decision is made, shall state any findings of fact and the reasons for the court's decision.

(7) After the court announces its decision, the justices' clerk shall as soon as practicable–

(a) make a record of any order made in the appropriate form in Schedule 1 to these Rules or, where there is no such form, in writing; and

(b) subject to paragraph (8), serve a copy of any order made on the parties to the proceedings and on any person with whom the child is living.

(8) Within 48 hours after the making of an order under section 48(4) or the making, ex parte, of–

(a) a prohibited steps order, or a specific issue order, under section 8, or

(b) an order under section 44, 48(9), 50, 75(1) or 102(1),

the applicant shall serve a copy of the order in the appropriate form in Schedule 1 to these Rules on–

(i) each party,

(ii) any person who has actual care of the child, or who had such care immediately prior to the making of the order, and

(iii) in the case of an order referred to in sub-paragraph (b), the local authority in whose area the child lives or is found.

PART III

MISCELLANEOUS

Costs

22.—(1) In any relevant proceedings, the court may, at any time during the proceedings in that court, make an order that a party pay the whole or any part of the costs of any other party.

(2) A party against whom the court is considering making a costs order shall have an opportunity to make representations as to why the order should not be made.

Confidentiality of documents

23.—(1) No document, other than a record of an order, held by the court and relating to relevant proceedings shall be disclosed, other than to–

(a) a party,

(b) the legal representative of a party,

(c) the guardian ad litem,

(d) the Legal Aid Board, or

(e) a welfare officer,

without leave of the justices' clerk or the court.

(2) Nothing in this rule shall prevent the notification by the court or the justices' clerk of a direction under section 37(1) to the authority concerned.

Enforcement of residence order

24. Where a person in whose favour a residence order is in force wishes to enforce it he shall file a written statement describing the alleged breach of the arrangements settled by the order, whereupon the justices' clerk shall fix a date, time and place for a hearing of the proceedings and give notice, as soon as practicable, to the person wishing to enforce the residence order and to any person whom it is alleged is in breach of the arrangements settled by that order, of the date fixed.

Notification of consent

25. Consent for the purposes of–

(a) section 16(3),

(b) section 33(7), or

(c) paragraph 19(1) of Schedule 2,

shall be given either–

(i) orally in court, or

(ii) in writing to the justices' clerk or the court and signed by the person giving his consent.

Secure accommodation

26. In proceedings under section 25, the justices' clerk shall, if practicable, arrange for copies of all written reports before the court to be made available before the hearing to–

(a) the applicant,

(b) the parent or guardian of the child,

(c) any legal representative of the child,

(d) the guardian ad litem, and

(e) the child, unless the justices' clerk or the court otherwise directs;

and copies of such reports may, if the court considers it desirable, be shown to any person who is entitled to notice of the proceedings in accordance with these Rules.

Investigation under section 37

27.—(1) This rule applies where a direction is given to an appropriate authority by a family proceedings court under section 37(1).

(2) On giving a direction the court shall adjourn the proceedings and the justices' clerk or the court shall record the direction in writing.

(3) A copy of the direction recorded under paragraph (2) shall, as soon as practicable after the direction is given, be served by the justices' clerk on the parties to the proceedings in which the direction is given and, where the appropriate authority is not a party, on that authority.

(4) When serving the copy of the direction on the appropriate authority the justices' clerk shall also serve copies of such of the documentary evidence which has been, or is to be, adduced in the proceedings as the court may direct.

(5) Where a local authority informs the court of any of the matters set out in section 37(3)(a) to (c) it shall do so in writing.

Limits on the power of a justices' clerk or a single justice to make an order under section 11(3) or section 38(1)

28. A justices' clerk or single justice shall not make an order under section 11(3) or section 38(1) unless–

(a) a written request for such an order has been made to which the other parties and any guardian ad litem consent and which they or their representatives have signed,

(b) a previous such order has been made in the same proceedings, and

(c) the terms of the order sought are the same as those of the last such order made.

Appeals to a family proceedings court under section 77(6) and paragraph 8(1) of Schedule 8

29.—(1) An appeal under section 77(6) or paragraph 8(1) of Schedule 8 shall be by application in accordance with rule 4.

(2) An appeal under section 77(6) shall be brought within 21 days from the date of the step to which the appeal relates.

Contribution orders

30.—(1) An application for a contribution order under paragraph 23(1) of Schedule 2 shall be accompanied by a copy of the contribution notice served in accordance with paragraph 22(1) of that Schedule and a copy of any notice served by the contributor under paragraph 22(8) of that Schedule.

(2) Where a local authority notifies the court of an agreement reached under paragraph 23(6) of Schedule 2, it shall do so in writing through the justices' clerk.

(3) An application for the variation or revocation of a contribution order under paragraph 23(8) of Schedule 2 shall be accompanied by a copy of the contribution order which it is sought to vary or revoke.

Direction to local education authority to apply for education supervision order

31.—(1) For the purposes of section 40(3) and (4) of the Education Act 1944**(a)**, a direction by a magistrates' court to a local education authority to apply for an education supervision order shall be given in writing.

(2) Where, following such a direction, a local education authority informs the court that they have decided not to apply for an education supervision order, they shall do so in writing.

Delegation by justices' clerk

32.—(1) In this rule, "employed as a clerk in court" has the same meaning as in rule 2(1) of the Justices' Clerks (Qualifications of Assistants) Rules 1979**(b)**.

(2) Anything authorised to be done by, to or before a justices' clerk under these Rules, or under paragraphs 13 to 15C of the Schedule to the Justices' Clerks Rules 1970**(c)** as amended by Schedule 3 to these Rules, may be done instead by, to or before a person employed as a clerk in court where that person is appointed by the magistrates' courts committee to assist him and where that person has been specifically authorised by the justices' clerk for that purpose.

(3) Any authorisation by the justices' clerk under paragraph (2) shall be recorded in writing at the time the authority is given or as soon as practicable thereafter.

Application of section 97 of the Magistrates' Courts Act 1980

33. Section 97 of the Magistrates' Courts Act 1980 shall apply to relevant proceedings in a family proceedings court as it applies to a hearing of a complaint under that section.

Consequential and minor amendments, savings and transitionals

34.—(1) Subject to paragraph (3) the consequential and minor amendments in Schedule 3 to these Rules shall have effect.

(2) Subject to paragraph (3), the provisions of the 1981 rules shall have effect subject to these Rules.

(a) 1944 c.31 (7 and 8 Geo.6); relevant amendments are made by paragraphs 8 to 10 of Schedule 13 to the Children Act 1989.
(b) S.I. 1979/570, amended by 1980/1897.
(c) S.I. 1970/231, amended by 1975/300, 1976/1767, 1978/754 and 1983/527.

(3) Nothing in these Rules shall affect any proceedings which are pending (within the meaning of paragraph 1 of Schedule 14 to the Act of 1989) immediately before these Rules come into force.

25th May 1991 *Mackay of Clashfern*, C.

SCHEDULE 1

FORMS

CHA 1. Application for a Parental Responsibility Order.

2. Parental Responsibility Order.

3. Application for the appointment of a guardian.

4. Order for the appointment of a guardian.

5. Application for the termination of an appointment of a guardian.

6. Order terminating the appointment of a guardian.

7. Contact/Residence Order.

8. Prohibited Steps Order.

9. Specific Issue Order.

10. Application for a Contact Order, Prohibited Steps Order, Residence Order or Specific Issue Order.

10A. Respondent's Answer to Section 10 Application.

11. Application to change child's surname.

11A. Application to remove child from the jurisdiction of the UK.

12. Order authorising change of child's surname/removal of child from the jurisdiction of the UK.

13. Application for Financial Provision.

13A. Respondent's Answer to Application for Financial Provision.

14. Statement of Means.

15. Application for variation/discharge of an order for financial provision.

16. Family Assistance Order.

17. Application for authority to hold a child in secure accommodation.

18. Order authorising child to be held in secure accommodation.

19. Application for a Care/Supervision Order.

20. Order for the care/supervision of a child.

21. Application for contact with a child in care.

22. Order allowing contact with a child in care.

23. Application for permission to refuse contact with a child in care.

24. Order refusing contact with a child in care.

25. Application for an Education Supervision Order.

26. Education Supervision Order.

27. Interim Care/Supervision Order.

28. Application to discharge Care/Supervision Order, vary Supervision Order or substitute Supervision Order for a Care Order.

29. Order discharging Care/Supervision Order, varying Supervision Order or substituting Supervision Order for a Care Order.

30. Order making or refusing the appointment of a guardian ad litem.

31. Order making or refusing the appointment of solicitor.

32. Application for a Child Assessment Order.

33. Child Assessment Order.

34. Application for an Emergency Protection Order.

35. Emergency Protection Order.

36. Application to vary Emergency Protection Order directions.

37. Order varying Emergency Protection Order directions.

38. Application to extend Emergency Protection Order.

39. Order extending an Emergency Protection Order.

40. Application to discharge an Emergency Protection Order.

41. Order discharging an Emergency Protection Order.

42. Order authorising search for another child.

43. Application for a Warrant under Section 48.

44. Warrant under Section 48.

45. Application for Recovery Order.

46. Recovery Order.

47. Order that a child attend proceedings.

47A. Order to a person to bring a child to court.

48. Order to a person to disclose whereabouts of a child.

49. Application to further extend a Supervision Order.

50. Order further extending a Supervision Order.

51. Application to extend an Education Supervision Order.

52. Order extending an Education Supervision Order.

53. Application to discharge an Education Supervision Order.

54. Order discharging an Education Supervision Order.

55. Application to vary or discharge an order or direction.

56. General Order Form.

57. Refusal of Order.

59. Form for the disclosure of address.

60. Application concerning registration of child minders or providers of day care.

61. Order concerning registration of child minders or providers of day care.

62. Application for a Warrant under Section 102.

63. Warrant under Section 102.

64. Certificate of Transfer.

65. Refusal to Transfer Proceedings.

SCHEDULE 2

RESPONDENTS AND NOTICE

(i) *Provision under which proceedings brought*	(ii) *Minimum number of days prior to hearing or directions appointment for service under rule 4(1)(b)*	(iii) *Respondents*	(iv) *Persons to whom notice is to be given*
All applications.	See separate entries below.	Subject to separate entries below, every person whom the applicant believes to have parental responsibility for the child; where the child is the subject of a care order, every person whom the applicant believes to have had parental responsibility immediately prior to the making of the care order; in the case of an application to extend, vary or discharge an order, the parties to the proceedings leading to the order which it is sought to have extended, varied or discharged; in the case of specified proceedings, the child.	Subject to separate entries below, the local authority providing accommodation for the child; persons who are caring for the child at the time when the proceedings are commenced; in the case of proceedings brought in respect of a child who is alleged to be staying in a refuge which is certificated under section 51(1) or (2), the person who is providing the refuge.
Section 8 or Schedule 1.	21 days	As for "all applications" above, and: in the case of proceedings under Schedule 1, those persons whom the applicant believes to be interested in or affected by the proceedings.	As for "all applications" above, and: in the case of an application for a section 8 order, every person whom the applicant believes– (i) to be named in a court order with respect to the same child, which has not ceased to have effect, (ii) to be a party to pending proceedings in respect of the same child, or (iii) to be a person with whom the child has lived for at least 3 years prior to the application, unless, in a case to which (i) or (ii) applies, the applicant believes that the court order or pending proceedings are not relevant to the application.

(i) *Provision under which proceedings brought*	(ii) *Minimum number of days prior to hearing or directions appointment for service under rule 4(1)(b)*	(iii) *Respondents*	(iv) *Persons to whom notice is to be given*
Section 4(1)(a), 4(3), 5(1), 6(7), 13(1), 16(6), 33(7), 77(6), paragraph 19(1), 23(1) or 23(8) of Schedule 2, paragraph 8(1) of Schedule 8, or paragraph 11(3) or 16(5) of Schedule 14.	14 days	Except for proceedings under section 77(6), Schedule 2, or paragraph 8(1) of Schedule 8, as for "all applications" above, and: in the case of an application under paragraph 11(3)(b) or 16(5) of Schedule 14, any person, other than the child, named in the order or directions which it is sought to discharge or vary; in the case or proceedings under section 77(6), the local authority against whose decision the appeal is made; in the case of an application under paragraph 23(1) of Schedule 2, the contributor; in the case of an application under paragraph 23(8) of Schedule 2– (i) if the applicant is the local authority, the contributor, and (ii) if the applicant is the contributor, the local authority. In the case of an application under paragraph 8(1) of Schedule 8, the local authority against whose decision the appeal is made.	As for "all applications" above, and: in the case of an application under paragraph 19(1) of Schedule 2, the parties to the proceedings leading to the care order; in the case of an application under section 5(1), the father of the child if he does not have parental responsibility.
Section 36(1), 39(1), 39(2), 39(3), 39(4), 43(1), or paragraph 6(3), 15(2) or 17(1) of Schedule 3.	7 days	As for "all applications" above, and: in the case of an application under section 39(2) or (3), the supervisor; in the case of proceedings under paragraph 17(1) of Schedule 3, the local education authority concerned; in the case of proceedings under section 36 or paragraph 15(2) or 17(1) of Schedule 3, the child.	As for "all applications" above, and: in the case of an application for an order under section 43(1)– (i) every person whom the applicant believes to be a parent of the child, (ii) every person whom the applicant believes to be caring for the child, (iii) every person in whose favour a contact order is in force with respect to the child, and

(i) *Provision under which proceedings brought*	(ii) *Minimum number of days prior to hearing or directions appointment for service under rule 4(1)(b)*	(iii) *Respondents*	(iv) *Persons to whom notice is to be given*
			(iv) every person who is allowed to have contact with the child by virtue of an order under section 34.
Section 31, 34(2), 34(3), 34(4), 34(9) or 38(8)(b).	3 days	As for "all applications" above, and: in the case of an application under section 34, the person whose contact with the child is the subject of the application.	As for "all applications" above, and: in the case of an application under section 31– (i) every person whom the applicant believes to be a party to pending relevant proceedings in respect of the same child, and (ii) every person whom the applicant believes to be a parent without parental responsibility for the child.
Section 43(12).	2 days	As for "all applications" above.	Those of the persons referred to in section 43(11)(a) to (e) who were not party to the application for the order which it is sought to have varied or discharged.
Section 25, 44(1), 44(9)(b), 45(4), 45(8), 46(7), 48(9), 50(1), 75(1) or 102(1).	1 day	Except for applications under section 75(1) or 102(1), as for "all applications" above, and: in the case of an application under section 44(9)(b) (i) the parties to the application for the order in respect of which it is sought to vary the directions; (ii) any person who was caring for the child prior to the making of the order; and (iii) any person whose contact with the child is affected by the direction which it is sought to have varied; in the case of an application under section 50, the person whom the applicant alleges to have effected or to have been or to be responsible for the taking or keeping of the child;	As for "all applications" above, and: in the case of an application under section 44(1), every person whom the applicant believes to be a parent of the child; in the case of an application under section 44(9)(b)– (i) the local authority in whose area the child is living, and (ii) any person whom the applicant believes to be affected by the direction which it is sought to have varied.

(i) *Provision under which proceedings brought*	(ii) *Minimum number of days prior to hearing or directions appointment for service under rule 4(1)(b)*	(iii) *Respondents*	(iv) *Persons to whom notice is to be given*
		in the case of an application under section 75(1), the registered person; in the case of an application under section 102(1), the person referred to in section 102(1) and any person preventing or likely to prevent such a person from exercising powers under enactments mentioned in subsection (6) of that section.	

SCHEDULE 3

Rule 34(1)

CONSEQUENTIAL AND MINOR AMENDMENTS

In the Justices' Clerks Rules 1970**(a)**, for paragraphs 13, 14 and 15 of the Schedule there shall be substituted the following paragraphs:

"**13.** The transfer of proceedings in accordance with any order made by the Lord Chancellor under Part I of Schedule 11.

14. The appointing of a guardian ad litem or solicitor for a child under section 41 of the Children Act 1989.

15. The giving, variation or revocation of directions in accordance with rule 14 of the Family Proceedings Courts (Children Act 1989) Rules 1991.

15A. The making of an order, in accordance with rule 28 of the Family Proceedings Courts (Children Act 1989) Rules 1991, under sections 11(3) or 38(1) of the Children Act 1989.

15B. By virtue of rule 33 of the Family Proceedings Courts (Children Act 1989) Rules 1991, the issuing of a witness summons under section 97 of the Magistrates' Courts Act 1980 in relevant proceedings, within the meaning of section 93(3) of the Children Act 1989.

15C. The requesting of a welfare report under section 7 of the Children Act 1989.".

(a) S.I. 1970/231, amended by S.I. 1975/300, 1976/1767, 1978/754 and 1983/527.

EXPLANATORY NOTE

(This note is not part of the Rules)

These Rules are made as a consequence of the passing of the Children Act 1989 (c.41) and set out the procedures to be followed in family proceedings courts in public and private law proceedings in which any question with respect to a child arises.

Rule 4 replaces the complaint and summons procedure by which proceedings related to children were formerly brought, by a procedure for instituting such proceedings by the making of an application, endorsed by the justices' clerk and returned to the applicant to be served by him, in accordance with rule 8, on the respondents who are listed in the third column of Schedule 2 to the rules. In addition, the applicant is required to give written notice to the persons listed in the fourth column of Schedule 2 to the rules in relation to the proceedings in question. Rule 4 also provides that certain applications may, with leave of the justices' clerk, be made ex parte.

Rule 6 provides a procedure for transferring the proceedings to another family proceedings court or to a county court in accordance with any Order made by the Lord Chancellor under Part I of Schedule 11 to the Act of 1989.

Rule 10 requires the justices' clerk or the court, in specified proceedings, to consider whether to appoint a guardian ad litem and rule 11 provides for the powers and duties of any guardian ad litem appointed. Rule 12 provides for the duties of a solicitor appointed by the court or by the guardian ad litem.

Rule 14 introduces a new type of preliminary hearing known as a "directions appointment" which may be held at any time during the proceedings, by the justices' clerk, a single justice or the full court with a view to issuing directions on the conduct of the proceedings. Rule 16 makes attendance by parties at directions appointments mandatory.

Rule 17 requires a party to file and serve on other parties written statements of the oral evidence which that party intends to adduce, and copies of any documents upon which the party intends to rely, at a hearing or directions appointment.

Rules 22 to 33 deal with miscellaneous matters such as appeals to family proceedings courts against decisions of local authorities and the delegation by justices' clerks of responsibilities imposed upon them under the rules.

Schedule 1 to the rules contains the forms of application and order which are prescribed by the rules. Schedule 2 contains a list of respondents and notice requirements for particular proceedings. Schedule 3 makes consequential and minor amendments to the Justices' Clerks Rules 1970.

Nothing in these Rules affects proceedings which are pending (within the meaning of paragraph 1 of Schedule 14 to the Act of 1989) immediately before these Rules come into force. These Rules come into force on 14th October 1991.

PRESCRIBED ORDERS – NORTHERN IRELAND, GUERNSEY AND THE ISLE OF MAN REGULATIONS

STATUTORY INSTRUMENTS

1991 No. 2032

CHILDREN AND YOUNG PERSONS

The Children (Prescribed Orders — Northern Ireland, Guernsey and Isle of Man) Regulations 1991

Made - - - -	*9th September 1991*
Laid before Parliament	*12th September 1991*
Coming into force	*14th October 1991*

The Secretary of State for Health, in exercise of the powers conferred by section 101 of the Children Act 1989(**a**), and of all other powers enabling him in that behalf, hereby makes the following Regulations:–

Citation, commencement, interpretation and extent

1.—(1) These Regulations may be cited as the Children (Prescribed Orders — Northern Ireland, Guernsey and Isle of Man) Regulations 1991 and shall come into force on 14th October 1991.

(2) In these Regulations unless the context requires otherwise—

"the Act" means the Children Act 1989;

"the authority" means the local authority(**b**) in whose care the child is by virtue of a care order under the Act;

"the Board" means a Health and Social Services Board in Northern Ireland established under article 16 of the Health and Personal Social Services (Northern Ireland) Order 1972(**c**);

"the Children Board" means the States Children Board in Guernsey;

"the Department" means the Department of Health and Social Security of the Isle of Man;

"the Northern Ireland Act" means the Children and Young Persons Act (Northern Ireland) 1968(**d**);

"the Act of Tynwald" means the Children and Young Persons Act 1966 (an Act of Tynwald)(**e**).

(3) In these Regulations, unless the context requires otherwise, any reference to a numbered regulation is to the regulation in these Regulations bearing that number and any reference in any regulation to a numbered paragraph is to the paragraph of that regulation bearing that number.

(4) This regulation and regulations 2, 6 and 8 shall extend to Northern Ireland.

(**a**) 1989 c.41. *See* the definition of "prescribed" in section 105(1).
(**b**) "local authority" is defined in section 105 (1) of the Act as the council of a county, a metropolitan district, a London Borough of the Common Council of the City of London; pursuant to section 2 of the Local Authority Social Services Act 1970 (c.42), local authority functions under the Children Act 1989 stand referred to the social services committee of a local authority.
(**c**) S.I. 1972/1265 (N.I.14).
(**d**) 1968 c.34.
(**e**) Vol. XX p.89; sections 2 and 3 are amended by the Children and Young Persons Act 1990 (c.13) (an Act of Tynwald).

Transfer of care orders from England and Wales to Northern Ireland

2.—(1) A care order being an order made by a court in England and Wales, which appears to the Secretary of State to correspond in its effect to an order which may be made under a provision in force in Northern Ireland, shall in the circumstances prescribed in paragraph (2) have effect for all the purposes of the Northern Ireland Act as if it were an order under section 95(1)(b) of that Act committing the child to the care of the Board for the area in which it is proposed that he will live.

(2) The circumstances referred to in paragraph (1) are that the court has given its approval under paragraph 19(1) of Schedule 2 to the Act to the authority arranging or assisting in arranging for the child to live in Northern Ireland.

(3) The care order shall cease to have effect for the purposes of the law of England and Wales if the following conditions are satisfied–

(a) the Board for the area in which the child will live in Northern Ireland has notified the court referred to in paragraph (2) in writing that it agrees to take over the care of the child; and

(b) the authority has notified the court referred to in paragraph (2) that it agrees to the Board taking over the care of the child.

Transfer of care orders to England and Wales from the Isle of Man

3.—(1) A relevant order within the meaning of section 56(6) of the Act of Tynwald (being an order made by a court in the Isle of Man which appears to the Secretary of State to correspond in its effect to an order which may be made under the Act) shall in the circumstances prescribed in paragraph (2) have effect for all the purposes of the Act in England and Wales as if it were a care order under section 31 of the Act placing the child in question in the care of the local authority in whose area he is to live.

(2) The circumstances prescribed are–

(a) that the relevant order was made otherwise than on a finding of guilt;

(b) that either–

(i) the court has given leave under sub-section (2) of section 56 of the Act of Tynwald for the Department to make arrangements for the child to be received into the care of that authority; or

(ii) the court has directed under sub-section (5) of that section that the said sub-section (2) shall not apply in relation to the order in question; and

(c) that the authority has agreed in writing to receive the child into its care.

Transfer of care orders from England and Wales to the Isle of Man

4. The conditions prescribed for the purposes of section 101(4) of the Act (child in care taken to live in the Isle of Man) in the case of a child who is taken to live in the Isle of Man are that–

(a) the court has given its approval under paragraph 19(1) of Schedule 2 to the Act to the authority arranging or assisting in arranging for the child to live in the Isle of Man;

(b) the Department has notified the court referred to in paragraph (a) in writing that it agrees to receive the child into its care; and

(c) the authority has notified the court referred to in paragraph (a) that it agrees to the Department receiving the child into care.

Transfer of care orders from England and Wales to Guernsey

5. The conditions prescribed for the purposes of section 101(4) of the Act in the case of a child who is taken to live in Guernsey are that–

(a) the court has given its approval under paragraph 19(1) of the Schedule 2 to the Act to the authority arranging or assisting in arranging for the child to live in care in Guernsey;

(b) the Children Board has notified the Guernsey Juvenile Court in writing that it agrees to receive the child into its care; and

(c) the authority has notified the Guernsey Juvenile Court that it agrees to the Children Board receiving the child into care; and

(d) the Guernsey Juvenile Court has made a fit person order in respect of the child.

Transfer of recovery orders from England and Wales to Northern Ireland

6.—(1) Where an authority has reason to believe that a child has been unlawfully taken to, or is being unlawfully kept in, Northern Ireland, or has run away to Northern Ireland, or is missing and believed to be in Northern Ireland, a recovery order made by a court in England and Wales under section 50 of the Act (being an order which appears to the Secretary of State to correspond in its effect to an order which may be made under any provision in force in Northern Ireland) shall have effect for all purposes of the law of Northern Ireland as if it were an order made under section 50 of the Act by a magistrate's court within the meaning of the Magistrates' Courts (Northern Ireland) Order 1981(**a**).

(2) Where a child is subject to a recovery order which is to have effect in Northern Ireland as mentioned in paragraph (1), any reasonable expenses incurred by an authorised person within the meaning of section 50(7) of the Act shall be recoverable from the authority in whose care the child was.

Transfer of recovery orders to England and Wales from the Isle of Man

7.—(1) For all purposes of the Act in England and Wales a recovery order under section 98B of the Act of Tynwald (being an order made by a court in the Isle of Man which appears to the Secretary of State to correspond in its effect to an order which may be made under the Act) shall in the circumstances prescribed in paragraph (2) have effect as if it were a recovery order made under section 50 of the Act.

(2) The circumstances referred to in paragraph (1) are that section 98A of the Act of Tynwald applies to the child in question otherwise than by virtue of an order committing him to the care of the Department on a finding of guilt.

Amendments to Children and Young Persons Act 1969

8.—(1) The following consequential amendments shall be made to section 25 of the Children and Young Persons Act 1969(**b**) (transfers between England or Wales and Northern Ireland)–

(a) in subsection (1)–

(i) after the words "training school order" there shall be inserted the words "or by any order which has effect as if it were a fit person order";

(ii) for the words "as if it were a care order" to the end of that subsection there shall be substituted the words "in a case in which there was a fit person order (or an order having effect as if it were a fit person order), as if it were a care order under section 31 of the Children Act 1989 and in a case in which there was a training school order as if it were a supervision order imposing a residence requirement as mentioned in section 12AA of this Act."(**c**);

(b) in subsection (2)–

(i) after the words "committed by a care order" there shall be inserted the words "to which paragraph 36 of Schedule 14 to the Children Act (criminal care order transitional provisions) applies";

(ii) after the words "interim order" there shall be inserted the words "or who is to accommodate a person pursuant to a supervision order imposing a residence requirement as mentioned in section 12AA of this Act";

(iii) the words "or to the care of the Secretary of State" shall be omitted;

(iv) for "83(3)(a), 88(3), 90 and 91(3)" there shall be substituted "88(3) and 90";

(v) for the words "a fit person order" there shall be substituted the words "the supervision order";

(**a**) S.I. 1981/1674 (N.I.26).

(**b**) 1969 c.54. Section 25 is amended by paragraph 15 of Schedule 2 to the Health and Social Services and Social Security Adjudications Act 1983 (c.41.) and for Northern Ireland by article 3 of and Schedule 2 to S.R. & O. (N.I.) 1973/256, and articles 2(1) and 11(5) of and Schedule 1 to S.I. 1973/2163.

(**c**) Section 12AA of the Children and Young Persons Act 1969 was inserted by paragraph 23 of Schedule 12 to the Children Act 1989.

(c) in subsection (3)–

(i) the words "or the Ministry of Home Affairs" shall be omitted;

(ii) for the words "or care order" there shall be substituted the words ", care order or supervision order";

(iii) in paragraph (b) after the words "care order" there shall be inserted the words "or supervision order";

(iv) sub-paragraph (i) of paragraph (b) shall be omitted;

(d) in subsection (4) the words "or the Ministry of Home Affairs" and the word "Ministry" shall be omitted.

(2) The following consequential amendments shall be made to section 26 of the Children and Young Persons Act 1969 (**a**) (transfers between England or Wales and the Channel Islands or the Isle of Man)–

(a) in subsection (1) after the words "interim order" there shall be inserted "or as a supervision order imposing a residence requirement as mentioned in section 12AA of this Act" and at the end of the subsection there shall be inserted the words "and "care order" means an order made under section 31 of the Children Act 1989.";

(b) for the words in subsection (2) from ", subject to the following subsection" to the end of the subsection (3) there shall be substituted "be deemed to be the subject of a care order placing the child in the care of a named local authority or, where the relevant order was made as a criminal disposal in criminal proceedings, a supervision order imposing a residence requirement as mentioned in section 12AA of this Act with a requirement that the child be accommodated by a designated local authority."

Signed by authority of the Secretary of State for Health

Virginia Bottomley
Minister of State,
Department of Health

9th September 1991

(**a**) Relevant designations of orders under section 26 of the Children and Young Persons Act 1969 (c.54) are made by the Children and Young Persons (Designation of Isle of Man Orders) Order 1991 (S.I. 1991/2031), the Children and Young Persons (Designation of Guernsey Order) Order 1971 (S.I. 1971/348) and the Children and Young Persons (Designation of Jersey Orders) Order 1972 (S.I. 1972/1074).

EXPLANATORY NOTE

(This note is not part of the Regulations)

These Regulations provide for orders which appear to the Secretary of State to be equivalent to orders available in Northern Ireland, the Isle of Man or the Channel Islands to have effect in certain circumstances there and to cease to have effect in England and Wales. Similarly, it provides that certain orders made in the Isle of Man may, in certain circumstances, have effect in England and Wales.

Regulation 2 provides that in certain circumstances a care order under the Children Act 1989 ("the 1989 Act") may have effect in Northern Ireland as if it were made in Northern Ireland.

Regulation 3 provides that in certain circumstances a care order made in the Isle of Man other than on a criminal conviction may have effect in England and Wales as if it were a care order made under section 31 of the 1989 Act.

Regulations 4 and 5 provide for the transfer of a child in care under section 31 to the care of the Department of Health and Social Security in the Isle of Man or the States Children Board in Guernsey respectively, subject to certain conditions being met, and for orders under section 31 to cease to have effect.

Regulation 6 provides for a recovery order under section 50 of the 1989 Act to have effect in Northern Ireland in certain circumstances. The local authority in England and Wales responsible for the child is responsible for the reasonable expenses incurred in Northern Ireland by persons authorised under the order so as to recover the child.

Regulation 7 provides for a recovery order made in the Isle of Man other than on a criminal conviction to have effect as if it were a recovery order under section 50 of the 1989 Act.

Regulation 8 makes consequential amendments to sections 25 and 26 of the Children and Young Persons Act 1969 (transfers between England or Wales and Northern Ireland, the Channel Islands or the Isle of Man).

SECURE ACCOMMODATION (NO. 2) REGULATIONS

STATUTORY INSTRUMENTS

1991 No. 2034

CHILDREN AND YOUNG PERSONS

The Children (Secure Accommodation) (No. 2) Regulations 1991

Made - - - -	*6th September 1991*
Laid before Parliament	*12th September 1991*
Coming into force -	*14th October 1991*

The Secretary of State for Health, in exercise of the powers conferred by section 25(2)(c) of the Children Act 1989**(a)** and of all other powers enabling him in that behalf hereby makes the following Regulations:

Citation and Commencement

1.—(1) These Regulations may be cited as the Children (Secure Accommodation) (No. 2) Regulations 1991 and shall come into force on 14th October 1991 immediately after the Children (Secure Accommodation) Regulations 1991**(b)**.

Applications to court – special cases

2.—(1) Applications to a court under section 25 of the Children Act 1989 in respect of a child provided with accommodation by a health authority, a National Health Service trust established under section 5 of the National Health Service and Community Care Act 1990**(c)** or a local education authority shall, unless the child is looked after by a local authority, be made only by the health authority, National Health Service trust or local education authority providing accommodation for the child.

(2) Applications to a court under section 25 of the Children Act 1989 in respect of a child provided with accommodation in a residential care home, nursing home or mental nursing home shall, unless the child is looked after by a local authority, be made only by the person carrying on the home in which accommodation is provided for the child.

Signed by authority of the Secretary of State for Health.

Virginia Bottomley
Minister of State,
Department of Health

6th September 1991

(a) 1989 c.41. Regulation 7 of the Children (Secure Accommodation) Regulations 1991 (S.I. 1991/1505) modifies section 25(2)(c) of the Children Act 1989 in relation to children referred to in regulation 2 of these Regulations.
(b) S.I. 1991/1505.
(c) 1990 c.19.

EXPLANATORY NOTE

(This note is not part of the Regulations)

These Regulations make provision for applications to the court under section 25 of the Children Act 1989 (secure accommodation) in respect of children accommodated by health authorities, National Health Service trusts and local education authorities and children accommodated in residential care homes, nursing homes or mental nursing homes to be made as the case may be only by the health authority, National Health Service trust, local education authority, or person carrying on the residential care home, nursing home or mental nursing home unless the child in question is looked after by a local authority.

60p net

ISBN 0 11 015034 1

Printed in the United Kingdom for HMSO

879 WO1756 C38 9/91 452/3 4235 134976 913527

ANNEX E

COMMENCEMENT AND TRANSITIONAL PROVISIONS ORDER (SI 828)

STATUTORY INSTRUMENTS

1991 No. 828 (C.19)

CHILDREN AND YOUNG PERSONS

The Children Act 1989 (Commencement and Transitional Provisions) Order 1991

Made - - - - 25th March 1991

The Secretary of State for Health, in exercise of the powers conferred by section 108(2) and (8) of the Children Act 1989(**a**) and of all other powers enabling him in that behalf, hereby makes the following Order:

Citation

1. This Order may be cited as the Children Act 1989 (Commencement and Transitional Provisions) Order 1991.

Interpretation

2. In this Order "the Act" means the Children Act 1989.

Commencement

3.—(1) Paragraph 21 of Schedule 10 to the Act (adoption contact register) and section 88(1) of the Act so far as it relates to that paragraph shall come into force on 1st May 1991.

(2) All provisions of the Act which are not by then already in force shall come into force on 14th October 1991.

Modifications of transitional provisions

4. Schedule 14 to the Act shall have effect from 14th October 1991 subject to the additions and modifications set out in the Schedule to this Order.

William Waldegrave
Secretary of State for Health

25th March 1991

SCHEDULE

Article 4

ADDITIONS TO, AND MODIFICATIONS OF, SCHEDULE 14 TO THE ACT

1. In paragraph 16(4) for the words "sub-paragraph (5) only applies" there shall be substituted the words–

"sub-paragraphs (5) and (6) only apply".

2. In paragraph 16(5)–

(a) at the beginning of the sub-paragraph there shall be inserted–

"Subject to sub-paragraph (6),";

(b) after the word "shall" there shall be inserted–

", subject to the provisions of section 25 of this Act and of any regulations made under that section,"; and

(c) after the words "in this Act" there shall be inserted–

"other than section 25".

3. After sub-paragraph 16(5) there shall be inserted the following sub-paragraph–

"(6) Where directions referred to in sub-paragraph (5) are to the effect that a child be placed in accommodation provided for the purpose of restricting liberty then the directions shall cease to have effect upon the expiry of the maximum period specified by regulations under section 25(2)(a) in relation to children of his description, calculated from 14th October 1991."

4. In paragraph 16A(**a**)–

(a) after the number "16A." there shall be inserted "—(1)"; and

(b) after sub-paragraph (1) there shall be inserted–

"(2) Where immediately before the day on which Part IV commences a child was in the care of a local authority and as the result of an order–

(a) under section 7(2) of the Family Law Reform Act 1969; or

(b) made in the exercise of the High Court's inherent jurisdiction with respect to children,

continued to be in the care of a local authority and was made a ward of court, he shall on the day on which Part IV commences, cease to be a ward of court."

5. After paragraph 18 there shall be inserted the following paragraph–

"**18A.**—(1) This paragraph applies to any decision of a local authority to terminate arrangements for access or to refuse to make such arrangements–

(a) of which notice has been given under, and in accordance with, section 12B of the Child Care Act 1980 (termination of access); and

(b) which is in force immediately before the commencement of Part IV.

(2) On and after the commencement of Part IV, a decision to which this paragraph applies shall have effect as a court order made under section 34(4) authorising the local authority to refuse to allow contact between the child and the person to whom notice was given under section 12B of the Child Care Act 1980."

6. In paragraph 25(3) for the words "more than six months" there shall be substituted "six months or more".

(**a**) Paragraph 16A was inserted by paragraph 33(4) of Schedule 16 to the Courts and Legal Services Act 1990 (c.41).

EXPLANATORY NOTE

(This note is not part of the Order)

This Order brings into force on 1st May 1991 paragraph 21 of Schedule 10 to the Children Act 1989 which amends the Adoption Act 1976 (c.36) so as to establish an Adoption Contact Register to facilitate contact between an adopted person and any relative of his. The Order brings into force on 14th October 1991 all other provisions of the Children Act 1989 except those which have already been brought into force by section 108(2) of that Act.

Article 4 of, and the Schedule to, this order add to and modify the transitional provisions contained in Schedule 14 to the 1989 Act.

Paragraphs 2 and 3 make court directions relating to secure accommodation subject to the provisions of section 25 (secure accommodation) and any regulations made under that section and also to a new sub-paragraph 16(6) which provides that such directions shall cease to have effect after the maximum period specified by regulations under section 25(2).

Paragraph 4 adds a sub-paragraph to paragraph 16A (cessation of wardship where ward in care) to provide that wardship shall cease on the commencement of the Act where a child who was already in care was subsequently made a ward of court and remains in care.

Paragraph 5 adds a paragraph making provision for there to be a deemed order under section 34 of the Act (contact with child in care) where a local authority decision terminating access or refusing access was in force immediately before the Act comes into force.

Paragraphs 1 and 6 make minor amendments.

COMMENCEMENT NO.2 – AMENDMENTS AND TRANSITIONAL PROVISIONS ORDER (SI 1990)

STATUTORY INSTRUMENTS

1991 No. 1990 (C.56)

CHILDREN AND YOUNG PERSONS

The Children Act 1989 (Commencement No. 2—Amendment and Transitional Provisions) Order 1991

Made - - - - 4th September 1991

The Secretary of State for Health in exercise of the powers conferred by section 108(2) and (8) of the Children Act 1989(**a**) and of all other powers enabling him in that behalf, hereby makes the following Order:

Citation

1. This Order may be cited as the Children Act 1989 (Commencement No. 2—Amendment and Transitional Provisions) Order 1991.

Amendment of Order

2. The Children Act 1989 (Commencement and Transitional Provisions) Order 1991(**b**) shall be amended as follows–

(a) In article 3(2) (commencement), after the words "in force" there shall be inserted the words "except section 5(11) and (12) (appointment of guardians to children's estates),";

(b) After article 3(2) there shall be added to article 3 the following paragraph–

"(3) Section 5(11) and (12) of the Act shall come into force on 1 February 1992."

(c) The Schedule (additions to, and modifications of, Schedule 14 to the Children Act 1989) is amended with effect from 14 October 1991 in accordance with the Schedule to this Order.

Signed by authority of the Secretary of State for Health

Virginia Bottomley
4th September 1991 Minister of State, Department of Health

(**a**) 1989 c. 41.
(**b**) S.I. No. 1991/828.

SCHEDULE

Article 2(c)

AMENDMENTS TO THE SCHEDULE TO THE CHILDREN ACT 1989 (COMMENCEMENT AND TRANSITIONAL PROVISIONS) ORDER 1991

1. Before paragraph 1 there shall be inserted the following paragraphs–

"**1A.**—(1) In paragraph 1(1), for the words "Subject to sub-paragraph (4)" there shall be substituted "Subject to sub-paragraphs (1A) and (4)".

(2) After paragraph 1(1) there shall be inserted the following sub-paragraph–

"(1A) Proceedings pursuant to section 7(2) of the Family Law Reform Act 1969(**a**) (committal of wards of court to care of local authority) or in the exercise of the High Court's inherent jurisdiction with respect to children which are pending in relation to a child who has been placed or allowed to remain in the care of a local authority shall not be treated as pending proceedings after 13th October 1992 for the purposes of this Schedule if no final order has been made by that date pursuant to section 7(2) of the 1969 Act or in the exercise of the High Court's inherent jurisdiction in respect of the child's care."

1B.—(1) In paragraph 7(2), for the words "Parts I and II" there shall be substituted "Parts I and II and paragraph 15 of Schedule I".

(2) After paragraph 7(3)(c) there shall be inserted the following–

"(d) for paragraph 15 of Schedule I there shall be substituted–

"**15.** Where a child lives with a person as the result of a custodianship order within the meaning of section 33 of the Children Act 1975(**b**), a local authority may make contributions to that person towards the cost of the accommodation and maintenance of the child so long as that person continues to have legal custody of that child by virtue of the order."."

1C. References in paragraphs 12, 13 and 14 to the commencement of section 5 shall be construed as references to the commencement of sub-sections (1) to (10) and (13) of that section except in relation to the appointment of a guardian of the estate of any child in which case they shall be construed as a reference to the commencement of sub-sections (11) and (12) of that section.

1D. In paragraph 16 after sub-paragraph (3) there shall be inserted the following sub-paragraph–

"(3A) Where in respect of a child who has been placed or allowed to remain in the care of a local authority pursuant to section 7(2) of the Family Law Reform Act 1969 or in the exercise of the High Court's inherent jurisdiction and the child is still in the care of a local authority, proceedings have ceased by virtue of paragraph 1 (1A) to be treated as pending, paragraph 15(2) shall apply on 14th October 1992 as if the child was in care pursuant to an order as specified in paragraph 15(1)(e)(ii) or (h) as the case may be."."

2. For paragraph 4 there shall be substituted–

"**4.** In paragraph 16A(**c**)–

(a) after the number "16A." there shall be inserted "—(1)"; and

(b) after sub-paragraph (1) there shall be inserted–

"(2) Where immediately before the day on which Part IV commences a child was in the care of a local authority and as a result of an order–

(a) pursuant to section 7(2) of the Family Law Reform Act 1969; or

(b) made in the exercise of the High Court's inherent jurisdiction with respect to children,

continued to be in the care of a local authority and was made a ward of court, he shall on the day on which Part IV commences, cease to be a ward of court.

(3) Sub-paragraphs (1) and (2) do not apply in proceedings which are pending."."

(**a**) 1969 c. 46.
(**b**) 1975 c. 72.
(**c**) Paragraph 16A was inserted by paragraph 33(4) of Schedule 16 to the Courts and Legal Services Act 1990 (c. 41).

EXPLANATORY NOTE

(This note is not part of the Regulations)

This Order postpones the coming into force of section 5(11) and (12) of the Children Act 1989 from 14th October 1991 to 1st February 1992. Those provisions concern the appointment of guardians to children's estates.

Article 2 and the Schedule to the Order amend the schedule to the Children Act 1989 (Commencement and Transitional Provisions) Order 1991 ("the first Order") so as to further add to and modify the transitional provisions contained in Schedule 14 to the Children Act 1989 as follows:–

Paragraph 1 inserts four new paragraphs before the first paragraph of the Schedule to the first Order. Paragraph 1A amends the provisions governing "pending proceedings" in paragraph 1 of Schedule 14 to the 1989 Act to restrict to one year the period for which proceedings in respect of a child who has been placed or allowed to remain in the care of the local authority pursuant to section 7(2) of the Family Law Reform Act 1969 or in the exercise of the inherent jurisdiction can be pending. Paragraph 1B allows local authorities to continue to make contributions towards the maintenance of a child living with a person as the result of a custodianship order so long as the order lasts. Paragraph 1C makes transitional provisions necessary as a result of the deferment of the coming into force of section 5(11) and (12). Paragraph 1D makes provision for the orders in proceedings which are treated in consequence of paragraph 1A as no longer pending to be treated as care orders under the 1989 Act.

Paragraph 2 makes modifications to paragraph 4 of the first Order as a consequence of the amendment to the provisions governing "pending proceedings".

NOTE AS TO EARLIER COMMENCEMENT ORDERS

Under section 108(2) of the Children Act 1989, sections 89 and 96(3) to (7), and paragraph 35 of Schedule 12 came into force on 16th November 1989 and paragraph 36 of Schedule 12 came into force on 16th January 1990. By S.I. 1991/828, paragraph 1 of Schedule 10 (adoption contact register) and section 88(1) (for purposes related to that paragraph) came into force on 1st May 1991 and all other provisions of the Act (other than those the commencement of which is postponed by this Order) come into force on 14th October 1991.

ANNEX G

AMENDMENTS TO THE ACT CARRIED IN THE COURTS AND LEGAL SERVICES ACT 1990 AND THE NHS AND COMMUNITY CARE ACT 1990

CLS 1990 – Courts and Legal Services Act 1990
NHS & CC 1990 – National Health Service and Community Care Act 1990

Section/ Schedule	*Amendments made*	*Effected by*
S15(1)	Insert "section 6 of the Family Law Reform Act 1969" after "provisions of"	CLS 1990 Sch 16 para 10(1)
S21(2)(c)(i)	Insert "16(3A) or" after "section"	CLS 1990 Sch 16 para 11
S21(3)	Insert "or otherwise made available pursuant to arrangements made by a District Health Authority" after the words "vested in the Secretary of State"	NHS & CC 1990 Sch 9 para 36(1)
S23(2)(e)	Insert "in accordance with arrangements made" after "provided"	CLS 1990 Sch 16 para 12(1)
S23(5)	Insert a new subsection after S23(5): "(5A) For the purposes of subsection (5) a child shall be regarded as living with a person if he stays with that person for a continuous period of more than 24 hours"	CLS 1990 Sch 16 para 12(2)
S24(2) (d)(ii)	Add at the end "or in any accommodation provided by a National Health Service trust"	NHS & CC 1990 Sch 9 para 36(2) (a)
S24(12)(c)	Add at the end "or any accommodation provided by a National Health Service trust"	NHS & CC 1990 Sch 9 para 36(2)(b)
S24(13)	Insert two new subsections after 23(13): "(14) every local authority shall establish a procedure for considering any representations (including any complaint) made to them by a person qualifying for advice and assistance about the discharge of their functions under this Part in relation to him. (15) In carrying out any consideration of representations under subsection (14) ,a local authority shall comply with any regulations made by the Secretary of State for the purposes of this subsection."	CLS 1990 Sch 16 para 13
S27(1)	Delete the words "or other person" and the words "or person"	CLS 1990 Sch 16 para 14(a)

Section/ Schedule	Amendments made	Effected by
S27(3)	Replace the word "persons" with the word "authorities" Insert "or National Health Service trust" after "health authority"	CLS 1990 Sch 16 para 14(b)
S29(8)(c)	Add at the end "or any other hospital made available pursuant to arrangements made by a District Health Authority"	NHS & CC 1990 Sch 9 para 36(3)
S29(9)	Replace the words "expenses reasonably" with the words "reasonable expenses"	CLS 1990 Sch 16 para 15
S37(5)(b)	Replace the words "does not reside" with the words "is not ordinarily resident"	CLS 1990 Sch 16 para 16
S41(11)	Insert a new subsection after 41(11): "(12) The Secretary of State may, with the consent of the Treasury, make such grants with respect to the expenditure of any local authority– (a) in connection with the establishment and administration of guardians ad litem panels in accordance with this section; (b) in paying expenses, fees, allowances and in the provision of training for members of such panels, as he considers appropriate."	CLS 1990 Sch 16 para 17
S42(1)(a)	Insert "or an authorised person" after "authority" Delete the word "or" at the end of the subparagraph	CLS 1990 Sch 16 para 18(2) CLS 1990 Sch 20
S42(1)(b)	Delete the word "other" Insert at the end of subsection (1)(b): "; or (c) any records of, or held by, an authorised person which were compiled in connection with the activities of that person, so far as those records relate to that child."	CLS 1990 Sch 16 para 18(3)
S42(3)	Insert a new subsection after 42(3): "(4) In this section "authorised person" has the same meaning as in section 31."	CLS 1990 Sch 16 para 18(4)

Section/ Schedule	*Amendments made*	*Effected by*
S45(10)	Replace section 45(10) with the following: "(10) No appeal may be made against– (a) the making of, or refusal to make, an emergency protection order; (b) the extension of, or refusal to extend the period during which such an order is to have effect; (c) the discharge of, or refusal to discharge, such an order; or (d) the giving of, or refusal to give, any direction in connection with such an order."	CLS 1990 Sch 16 para 19
S47(11)(d)	Insert "or National Health Service trust" after "health authority"	CLS 1990 Sch 16 para 20
S80(1)(d)	Insert "or National Health Service trust" after "health authority"	NHS & CC 1990 Sch 9 para 36(4) (a)
S80(5)(e)	Insert "National Health Service trust" after "health authority"	NHS & CC 1990 Sch 9 para 36(4)(b)
S81(1)(d)	Delete the word "registered"	CLS 1990 Sch 16 para 21
S81(1)(f)	Insert "in accordance with arrangements made" after "provided"	CLS 1990 Sch 16 para 21
S85(1)	Insert "National Health Service trust" after "health authority"	NHS & CC 1990 Sch 9 para 36(5)
S93(2)(f)	Replace the words "the United Kingdom" with the words "England and Wales"	CLS 1990 Sch 16 para 22(a)
S93(2)(g)	Insert "or resides" after "is"	CLS 1990 Sch 16 para 22(b)
S94(1)	Replace the first word "An" with the words "Subject to any express provisions to the contrary made by or under this Act, an"	CLS 1990 Sch 16 para 23
S97(8)	Replace the words "Section 71 of the Act of 1980 (newspaper reports of certain proceedings)" with the words "Sections 69 (sittings of magistrates' courts for family proceedings) and 71 (newspaper reports of certain proceedings) of the Act of 1980"	CLS 1990 Sch 16 para 24
S108(12)	In the entry relating to Schedule 14, delete "18"	CLS 1990 Sch 16 para 25

Section/ Schedule	Amendments made	Effected by
Sch 1 para 1(6)	Insert a new subparagraph after 1(6): "(7) Where a child is a ward of court, the court may exercise any of its powers under this Schedule even though no application has been made to it."	CLS 1990 Sch 16 para 10(2)
Sch 2 para 14(c)	Insert a new subparagraph after 14(c): "(d) the records kept by local authorities."	CLS 1990 Sch 16 para 26
Sch 3 para 7	Delete paragraph	CLS 1990 Sch 16 para 27
Sch 4 para 1(1), (2), (4), (5), (8) and (9)	Omit the word "voluntary" wherever it occurs in subparagraphs (1), (2), (4), (5), (8) and (9)	CLS 1990 Sch 16 para 28(1)
Sch 4 Para (6)(b)(i)	Delete the words "as a voluntary home"	CLS 1990 Sch 16 para 28(2)
Sch 6 Para 3(1)	Replace the word "Part" with the word "Schedule"	CLS 1990 Sch 16 para 29
Sch 9 para 2(1)	Insert at the end of subparagraph 2(1): "unless– (a) he has disclosed the fact to the appropriate local authority; and (b) obtained their written consent."	CLS 1990 Sch 16 para 30(2)
Sch 9 para 2(2)(g)	Replace "61" with "69"	CLS 1990 Sch 16 para 30(3)
Sch 12 para 25	Delete this paragraph	CLS 1990 Sch 16 para 31
Sch 13 para 24	Delete this paragraph	CLS 1990 Sch 16 para 2(2)
Sch 13 para 25	Delete this paragraph	CLS 1990 Sch 16 para 6(2)
Sch 13 para 40	Delete this paragraph	CLS 1990 Sch 16 para 32
Sch 14 para 15(1)(f)	Delete the word "or" at the end of the subparagraph	CLS 1990 Sch 20

Section/ Schedule	*Amendments made*	*Effected by*
Sch 14 para 15(1)(g)	Insert a new subparagraph after (1)(g): "; or– (h) in care by virtue of an order of the court made in the exercise of the High Court's inherent jurisdiction with respect to children."	CLS 1990 Sch 16 para 33(2)
Sch 14 para 16(4)	Replace the word "(g)" with the word "(h)"	CLS 1990 Sch 16 para 33(3) (a)
Sch 14 para 16(5)	Delete from "under" to "1973". Replace with the following: "(a) under section 4(4) (a) of the Guardianship Act 1973; (b) under section 43(5) (a) of the Matrimonial Causes Act 1973; or (c) in the exercise of the High Court's inherent jurisdiction with respect to children,"	CLS 1990 Sch 16 para 33(3)(b)
Sch 14 para 16	Insert a new paragraph after paragraph 16: *"Cessation of wardship where child in care* 16A. Where a child who is a ward of court is in care by virtue of– (a) An order under section 7(2) of the Family Law Reform Act 1969; or (b) an order made in the exercise of the High Court's inherent jurisdiction with respect to children, he shall, on the day on which Part IV commences, cease to be a ward of court."	CLS 1990 Sch 16 para 33(4)
Sch 14 para 22(a)	Replace the word "(g)" with the word "(h)"	CLS 1990 Sch 16 para 33(5)
Sch 14 para 36(5)(b)	Replace the words "subsection (4)" with the words "subsection (6)"	CLS 1990 Sch 16 para 33(6)

EMERGENCY PROTECTION ORDER REGULATIONS (SI 1414)

STATUTORY INSTRUMENTS

1991 No. 1414

CHILDREN AND YOUNG PERSONS

The Emergency Protection Order (Transfer of Responsibilities) Regulations 1991

Made - - - -	*19th June 1991*
Laid before Parliament	*26th June 1991*
Coming into force	*14th October 1991*

The Secretary of State for Health, in exercise of the powers conferred by section 52(3) and (4) and section 104(4) of the Children Act 1989**(a)** and of all other powers enabling him in that behalf, hereby makes the following Regulations:—

Citation and commencement

1. These Regulations may be cited as the Emergency Protection Order (Transfer of Responsibilities) Regulations 1991 and shall come into force on 14th October 1991.

Transfer of responsibilities under emergency protection orders

2. Subject to regulation 5 of these Regulations, where—

(a) an emergency protection order has been made with respect to a child;

(b) the applicant for the order was not the local authority within whose area the child is ordinarily resident; and

(c) that local authority are of the opinion that it would be in the child's best interests for the applicant's responsibilities under the order to be transferred to them,

that authority shall (subject to their having complied with the requirements imposed by regulation 3(1) of these Regulations) be treated, for the purposes of the Children Act 1989, as though they and not the original applicant had applied for, and been granted, the order.

Requirements to be complied with by local authorities

3.—(1) In forming their opinion under regulation 2(c) of these Regulations the local authority shall consult the applicant for the emergency protection order and have regard to the following considerations—

(a) the ascertainable wishes and feelings of the child having regard to his age and understanding;

(b) the child's physical, emotional and educational needs for the duration of the emergency protection order;

(c) the likely effect on him of any change in his circumstances which may be caused by a transfer of responsibilities under the order;

(d) his age, sex, family background;

(e) the circumstances which gave rise to the application for the emergency protection order;

(**a**) 1989 c.41.

(f) any directions of a court and other orders made in respect of the child;

(g) the relationship (if any) of the applicant for the emergency protection order to the child, and

(h) any plans which the applicant may have in respect of the child.

(2) The local authority shall give notice, as soon as possible after they form the opinion referred to in regulation 2(c), of the date and time of the transfer to—

(a) the court which made the emergency protection order,

(b) the applicant for the order, and

(c) those (other than the local authority) to whom the applicant for the order gave notice of it.

(3) A notice required under this regulation shall be given in writing and may be sent by post.

When responsibility under emergency protection order transfers

4. The time at which responsibility under any emergency protection order is to be treated as having been transferred to a local authority shall be the time stated as the time of transfer in the notice given in accordance with regulation 3 of these Regulations by the local authority to the applicant for the emergency protection order or the time at which notice is given to him under that regulation, whichever is the later.

Exception for children in refuges

5. These Regulations shall not apply where the child to whom the emergency protection order applies is in a refuge in respect of which there is in force a Secretary of State's certificate issued under section 51 of the Children Act 1989 (refuges for children at risk) and the person carrying on the home or, the foster parent providing the refuge, having taken account of the wishes and feelings of the child, has decided that the child should continue to be provided with the refuge for the duration of the order.

Signed by authority of the Secretary of State for Health

Virginia Bottomley,
Minister of State,
Department of Health

19th June 1991

EXPLANATORY NOTE

(This note does not form part of the Regulations)

These Regulations make provision for a local authority to be treated as though they and not the original applicant for an emergency protection order had applied for and been granted the order. They make provision for requirements to have been complied with before responsibility under the order is transferred and for the time the transfer is to be treated as effected. The Regulations do not apply when the child who is the subject of the order is in a refuge and the child is to continue to live there for the duration of the order.

60p net

ISBN 0 11 014414 7

Printed in the UK by HMSO
879/WO1276 C33 452/4 6/91 3209777 19542

ALLOCATION OF PROCEEDINGS ORDER (SI 1677) AND ASSOCIATED LCD/HO GUIDANCE

STATUTORY INSTRUMENTS

1991 No. 1677 (L.21)

FAMILY PROCEEDINGS

The Children (Allocation of Proceedings) Order 1991

Made - - - -	*20th June 1991*
Laid before Parliament	*1st August 1991*
Coming into force	*14th October 1991*

The Lord Chancellor, in exercise of the powers conferred on him by section 92(9) and (10) of, and Part I of Schedule 11 to, the Children Act 1989**(a)**, and of all other powers enabling him in that behalf, hereby makes the following Order:-

Citation, commencement and interpretation

1.—(1) This Order may be cited as the Children (Allocation of Proceedings) Order 1991 and shall come into force on 14th October 1991.

(2) In this Order, unless the context otherwise requires-

"child"–

(a) means, subject to sub-paragraph (b), a person under the age of 18 with respect to whom proceedings are brought, and

(b) where the proceedings are under Schedule 1, also includes a person who has reached the age of 18;

"London commission area" has the meaning assigned to it by section 2(1) of the Justices of the Peace Act 1979**(b)**;

"petty sessions area" has the meaning assigned to it by section 4 of the Justices of the Peace Act 1979**(c)**; and

"the Act" means the Children Act 1989, and a section, Part or Schedule referred to by number alone means the section, Part or Schedule so numbered in that Act.

Classes of county court

2. For the purposes of this Order there shall be the following classes of county court:

(a) divorce county courts, being those courts designated for the time being as divorce county courts by an order under section 33 of the Matrimonial and Family Proceedings Act 1984**(d)**;

(b) family hearing centres, being those courts set out in Schedule 1 to this Order;

(c) care centres, being those courts set out in column (ii) of Schedule 2 to this Order.

(a) 1989 c.41. **(b)** 1979 c.55. **(c)** Section 4 was amended by the Local Government Act 1985 (c.51), section 12. **(d)** 1984 c.42.

Proceedings to be commenced in magistrates' court

3.—(1) Subject to paragraphs (2) and (3) and to article 4, proceedings under any of the following provisions shall be commenced in a magistrates' court:

(a) section 25 (use of accommodation for restricting liberty);

(b) section 31 (care and supervision orders);

(c) section 33(7) (leave to change name of or remove from United Kingdom child in care);

(d) section 34 (parental contact);

(e) section 36 (education supervision orders);

(f) section 43 (child assessment orders);

(g) section 44 (emergency protection orders);

(h) section 45 (duration of emergency protection orders etc.);

(i) section 46(7) (application for emergency protection order by police officer);

(j) section 48 (powers to assist discovery of children etc.);

(k) section 50 (recovery orders);

(l) section 75 (protection of children in an emergency);

(m) section 77(6) (appeal against steps taken under section 77(1));

(n) section 102 (powers of constable to assist etc.);

(o) paragraph 19 of Schedule 2 (approval of arrangements to assist child to live abroad);

(p) paragraph 23 of Schedule 2 (contribution orders);

(q) paragraph 8 of Schedule 8 (certain appeals);

(r) section 21 of the Adoption Act 1976**(a)**.

(2) Notwithstanding paragraph (l) and subject to paragraph (3), proceedings of a kind set out in sub-paragraph (b), (e), (f), (g), (i) or (j) of paragraph (1), and which arise out of an investigation directed, by the High Court or a county court, under section 37(1), shall be commenced–

(a) in the court which directs the investigation, where that court is the High Court or a care centre, or

(b) in such care centre as the court which directs the investigation may order.

(3) Notwithstanding paragraphs (l) and (2), proceedings of a kind set out in sub-paragraph (a) to (k), (n) or (o) of paragraph (l) shall be made to a court in which are pending other proceedings, in respect of the same child, which are also of a kind set out in those sub-paragraphs.

Application to extend, vary or discharge order

4.—(1) Subject to paragraphs (2) and (3), proceedings under the Act, or under the Adoption Act 1976-

(a) to extend, vary or discharge an order, or

(b) the determination of which may have the effect of varying or discharging an order,

shall be made to the court which made the order.

(2) Notwithstanding paragraph (1), an application for an order under section 8 which would have the effect of varying or discharging an order made, by a county court, in accordance with section 10(l)(b) shall be made to a divorce county court.

(3) Notwithstanding paragraph (1), an application to extend, vary or discharge an order made, by a county court, under section 38, or for an order which would have the effect of extending, varying or discharging such an order, shall be made to a care centre.

(a) 1976 c.36; a new section 21 was substituted by paragraph 9 of Schedule 10 to the Children Act 1989 (c.41).

(4) A court may transfer proceedings made in accordance with paragraph (l) to any other court in accordance with the provisions of articles 5 to 13.

TRANSFER OF PROCEEDINGS

Disapplication of enactments about transfer

5. Sections 38 and 39 of the Matrimonial and Family Proceedings Act 1984**(a)** shall not apply to proceedings under the Act or under the Adoption Act 1976.

Transfer from one magistrates' court to another

6. A magistrates' court (the "transferring court") shall transfer proceedings under the Act or under the Adoption Act 1976 to another magistrates' court (the "receiving court") where-

(a) having regard to the principle set out in section 1(2), the transferring court considers that the transfer is in the interests of the child-

(i) because it is likely significantly to accelerate the determination of the proceedings,

(ii) because it would be appropriate for those proceedings to be heard together with other family proceedings which are pending in the receiving court, or

(iii) for some other reason, and

(b) the receiving court, by its justices' clerk (as defined by rule 1(2) of the Family Proceedings Courts (Children Act 1989) Rules 1991**(b)**), consents to the transfer.

Transfer from magistrates' court to county court by magistrates' court

7.—(1) Subject to paragraphs (2), (3) and (4) and to articles 15 to 18, a magistrates' court may, upon application by a party or of its own motion, transfer to a county court proceedings of any of the kinds mentioned in article 3(1) where it considers it in the interests of the child to do so having regard, first, to the principle set out in section 1(2) and, secondly, to the following questions:

(a) whether the proceedings are exceptionally grave, important or complex, in particular-

(i) because of complicated or conflicting evidence about the risks involved to the child's physical or moral well-being or about other matters relating to the welfare of the child;

(ii) because of the number of parties;

(iii) because of a conflict with the law of another jurisdiction;

(iv) because of some novel and difficult point of law; or

(v) because of some question of general public interest;

(b) whether it would be appropriate for those proceedings to be heard together with other family proceedings which are pending in another court; and

(c) whether transfer is likely significantly to accelerate the determination of the proceedings, where–

(i) no other method of doing so, including transfer to another magistrates' court, is appropriate, and

(ii) delay would seriously prejudice the interests of the child who is the subject of the proceedings.

(2) Notwithstanding paragraph (1), proceedings of the kind mentioned in sub-paragraph (g) to (j), (1), (m), (p) or (q) of article 3(1) shall not be transferred from a magistrates' court.

(3) Notwithstanding paragraph (1), proceedings of the kind mentioned in sub-paragraph (a) or (n) of article 3(1) shall only be transferred from a magistrates' court to a county court in order to be heard together with other family proceedings which arise out of the same circumstances as gave rise to the proceedings to be transferred and which are pending in another court.

(a) 1984 c.42. **(b)** S.I. 1991/1395.

(4) Notwithstanding paragraphs (1) and (3), proceedings of the kind mentioned in article 3(1)(a) shall not be transferred from a magistrates' court which is not a family proceedings court within the meaning of section 92(1).

8. Subject to articles 15 to 18, a magistrates' court may transfer to a county court proceedings under the Act or under the Adoption Act 1976, being proceedings to which article 7 does not apply, where, having regard to the principle set out in section 1(2), it considers that in the interests of the child the proceedings can be dealt with more appropriately in that county court.

Transfer from magistrates' court following refusal of magistrates' court to transfer

9.—(1) Where a magistrates' court refuses to transfer proceedings under article 7, a party to those proceedings may apply to the care centre listed in column (ii) of Schedule 2 to this Order against the entry in column (i) for the petty sessions area or London commission area in which the magistrates' court is situated for an order under paragraph (2).

(2) Upon hearing an application under paragraph (1) the court may transfer the proceedings to itself where, having regard to the principle set out in section 1(2) and the questions set out in article 7(1)(a) to (c), it considers it in the interests of the child to do so.

(3) Upon hearing an application under paragraph (1) the court may transfer the proceedings to the High Court where, having regard to the principle set out in section 1(2), it considers–

(a) that the proceedings are appropriate for determination in the High Court, and

(b) that such determination would be in the interests of the child.

Transfer from one county court to another

10. Subject to articles 15 to 17, a county court (the "transferring court") shall transfer proceedings under the Act or under the Adoption Act 1976 to another county court (the "receiving court") where–

(a) the transferring court, having regard to the principle set out in section 1(2), considers the transfer to be in the interests of the child, and

(b) the receiving court is–

(i) of the same class or classes, within the meaning of article 2, as the transferring court, or

(ii) to be presided over by a judge or district judge who is specified by directions under section 9 of the Courts and Legal Services Act 1990**(a)** for the same purposes as the judge or district judge presiding over the transferring court.

Transfer from county court to magistrates' court by county court

11. A county court may transfer to a magistrates' court before trial proceedings which were transferred under article 7(1) where the county court, having regard to the principle set out in section 1(2) and the interests of the child, considers that the criterion cited by the magistrates' court as the reason for transfer–

(a) in the case of the criterion in article 7(1)(a), does not apply,

(b) in the case of the criterion in article 7(1)(b), no longer applies, because the proceedings with which the transferred proceedings were to be heard have been determined,

(c) in the case of the criterion in article 7(1)(c), no longer applies.

Transfer from county court to High Court by county court

12. A county court may transfer proceedings under the Act or the Adoption Act 1976 to the High Court where, having regard to the principle set out in section 1(2), it considers–

(a) 1990 c.41.

(a) that the proceedings are appropriate for determination in the High Court, and

(b) that such determination would be in the interests of the child.

Transfer from High Court to county court

13. Subject to articles 15, 16 and 18, the High Court may transfer to a county court proceedings under the Act or the Adoption Act 1976 where, having regard to the principle set out in section 1(2), it considers that the proceedings are appropriate for determination in such a court and that such determination would be in the interests of the child.

ALLOCATION OF PROCEEDINGS TO PARTICULAR COUNTY COURTS

Commencement

14. Subject to articles 18, 19 and 20 and to rule 2.40 of the Family Proceedings Rules 1991**(a)** (Application under Part I or II of the Children Act 1989 where matrimonial cause is pending), an application under the Act or under the Adoption Act 1976 which is to be commenced in a county court shall be commenced in a divorce county court.

Proceedings under Part I or II or Schedule 1

15.—(1) Subject to paragraph (3), where an application under Part I or II or Schedule 1 is to be transferred from a magistrates' court to a county court, it shall be transferred to a divorce county court.

(2) Subject to paragraph (3), where an application under Part I or II or Schedule 1, other than an application for an order under section 8, is to be transferred from the High Court to a county court, it shall be transferred to a divorce county court.

(3) Where an application under Part I or II or Schedule 1, other than an application for an order under section 8, is to be transferred to a county court for the purpose of consolidation with other proceedings, it shall be transferred to the court in which those other proceedings are pending.

Orders under section 8 of the Children Act 1989

16.—(1) An application for an order under section 8 in a divorce county court, which is not also a family hearing centre, shall, if the court is notified that the application will be opposed, be transferred for trial to a family hearing centre.

(2) Subject to paragraph (3), where an application for an order under section 8 is to be transferred from the High Court to a county court it shall be transferred to a family hearing centre.

(3) Where an application for an order under section 8 is to be transferred to a county court for the purpose of consolidation with other proceedings, it may be transferred to the court in which those other proceedings are pending whether or not it is a family hearing centre; but paragraph (l) shall apply to the application following the transfer.

Application for adoption or freeing for adoption

17.—(1) Subject to article 22, proceedings in a divorce county court, which is not also a family hearing centre, under section 12 or 18 of the Adoption Act 1976**(b)** shall, if the court is notified that the proceedings will be opposed, be transferred for trial to a family hearing centre.

(2) Where proceedings under the Adoption Act 1976 are to be transferred from a magistrates' court to a county court, they shall be transferred to a divorce county court.

Applications under Part III, IV or V

18.—(1) An application under Part III, IV or V, if it is to be commenced in a county court, shall be commenced in a care centre.

(a) S.I. 1991/1247. **(b)** 1976 c.36.

(2) An application under Part III, IV or V which is to be transferred from the High Court to a county court shall be transferred to a care centre.

(3) An application under Part III, IV or V which is to be transferred from a magistrates' court to a county court shall be transferred to the care centre listed against the entry in column (i) of Schedule 2 to this Order for the petty sessions area or London commission area in which the relevant magistrates' court is situated.

Principal Registry of the Family Division

19. The principal registry of the Family Division of the High Court shall be treated, for the purposes of this Order, as if it were a divorce county court, a family hearing centre and a care centre listed against every entry in column (i) of Schedule 2 to this Order (in addition to the entries against which it is actually listed).

Lambeth and Woolwich County Courts

20. Notwithstanding articles 14, 16 and 17, an application for an order under section 8 or under the Adoption Act 1976 may be commenced and tried in Lambeth County Court or in Woolwich County Court.

MISCELLANEOUS

Contravention of provision of this Order

21. Where proceedings are commenced or transferred in contravention of a provision of this Order, the contravention shall not have the effect of making the proceedings invalid; and no appeal shall lie against the determination of proceedings on the basis of such contravention alone.

Transitional provision – proceedings under Adoption Act 1976

22. Proceedings under the Adoption Act 1976 which are commenced in a county court prior to the coming into force of this Order may, notwithstanding article 17(1), remain in that court for trial.

20th June 1991 *Mackay of Clashfern, C.*

SCHEDULE I

FAMILY HEARING CENTRES

Midland and Oxford Circuit

Birmingham County Court
Coventry County Court
Derby County Court
Leicester County Court
Lincoln County Court
Mansfield County Court
Northampton County Court
Nottingham County Court
Oxford County Court
Peterborough County Court
Stafford County Court
Stoke-on-Trent County Court
Telford County Court
Walsall County Court
Wolverhampton County Court
Worcester County Court

Northern Circuit

Blackburn County Court
Bolton County Court
Carlisle County Court
Lancaster County Court
Liverpool County Court
Manchester County Court
Stockport County Court

North Eastern Circuit

Barnsley County Court
Bradford County Court
Darlington County Court
Dewsbury County Court
Doncaster County Court
Durham County Court
Halifax County Court
Harrogate County Court
Huddersfield County Court
Keighley County Court
Kingston-upon-Hull County Court
Leeds County Court
Newcastle-upon-Tyne County Court
Pontefract County Court
Rotherham County Court
Scarborough County Court
Sheffield County Court
Skipton County Court
Sunderland County Court
Teesside County Court
Wakefield County Court
York County Court

South Eastern Circuit

Brighton County Court
Bow County Court
Brentford County Court
Bromley County Court
Cambridge County Court
Canterbury County Court
Chelmsford County Court
Chichester County Court
Colchester and Clacton County Court
Croydon County Court
Edmonton County Court
Guildford County Court
Hitchin County Court
Ilford County Court
Ipswich County Court
Kingston-upon-Thames County Court
Luton County Court
Maidstone County Court
Medway County Court
Milton Keynes County Court
Norwich County Court
Reading County Court
Romford County Court
Slough County Court
Southend County Court
Wandsworth County Court
Watford County Court
Willesden County Court

Wales and Chester Circuit

Aberystwyth County Court
Caernarfon County Court
Cardiff County Court
Carmarthen County Court
Chester County Court
Crewe County Court
Haverfordwest County Court
Llangefni County Court
Macclesfeld County Court
Merthyr Tydfil County Court
Newport (Gwent) County Court
Rhyl County Court
Swansea County Court
Warrington County Court
Welshpool and Newtown County Court
Wrexham County Court

Western Circuit

Basingstoke County Court
Bournemouth County Court
Bristol County Court
Exeter County Court
Gloucester County Court
Plymouth County Court
Portsmouth County Court
Southampton County Court
Swindon County Court
Taunton County Court
Truro County Court

SCHEDULE 2

CARE CENTRES

(i) *Petty Sessions Areas*	*(ii)* *Care Centres*
	Midland and Oxford Circuit
Abingdon	Oxford County Court
Aldridge and Brownhills	Wolverhampton County Court
Alfreton and Belper	Derby County Court
Ashby-De-La-Zouch	Leicester County Court
Atherstone and Coleshill	Coventry County Court
Barton-on-Humber	Lincoln County Court
Bewdley and Stourport	Worcester County Court
Bicester	Oxford County Court
Birmingham	Birmingham County Court
Boston	Lincoln County Court
Bourne and Stamford	Lincoln County Court
Bridgnorth	Telford County Court
Brigg	Lincoln County Court
Bromsgrove	Worcester County Court
Burton-upon-Trent	Stoke-on-Trent County Court
Caistor	Lincoln County Court
Cannock	Wolverhampton County Court
Cambridge	Peterborough County Court
Cheadle	Stoke-on-Trent County Court
Chesterfield	Derby County Court
City of Hereford	Worcester County Court
Congleton	Stoke-on-Trent County Court
Corby	Northampton County Court
Coventry	Coventry County Court
Crewe and Nantwich	Stoke-on-Trent County Court
Daventry	Northampton County Court
Derby and South Derbyshire	Derby County Court
Didcot and Wantage	Oxford County Court
Drayton	Telford County Court
Dudley	Wolverhampton County Court
East Retford	Nottingham County Court
East Oxfordshire	Oxford County Court
Eccleshall	Stoke-on-Trent County Court
Elloes	Lincoln County Court
Ely	Peterborough County Court
Epworth and Goole	Lincoln County Court
Gainsborough	Lincoln County Court
Glossop	Derby County Court
Grantham	Lincoln County Court
Grimsby and Cleethorpes	Lincoln County Court
Halesowen	Wolverhampton County Court
Henley	Oxford County Court
High Peak	Derby County Court
Huntingdon	Peterborough County Court
Ilkeston	Derby County Court
Kettering	Northampton County Court
Kidderminster	Worcester County Court
Leek	Stoke-on-Trent County Court
Leicester (City)	Leicester County Court
Leicester (County)	Leicester County Court
Lichfield	Stoke-on-Trent County Court
Lincoln District	Lincoln County Court
Loughborough	Leicester County Court
Louth	Lincoln County Court
Ludlow	Telford County Court
Lutterworth	Leicester County Court
Malvern Hills	Worcester County Court
Mansfield	Nottingham County Court

(i) *Petty Sessions Areas*	*(ii)* *Care Centres*
Market Bosworth	Leicester County Court
Market Harborough	Leicester County Court
Market Rasen	Lincoln County Court
Melton and Belvoir	Leicester County Court
Mid-Warwickshire	Coventry County Court
Mid-Worcestershire	Worcester County Court
Newark and Southwell	Nottingham County Court
Newcastle-under-Lyme	Stoke-on-Trent County Court
Newmarket	Peterborough County Court or Ipswich County Court
Northampton	Northampton County Court
North Herefordshire	Worcester County Court
North Oxfordshire and Chipping Norton	Oxford County Court
North Witchford	Peterborough County Court
Nottingham	Nottingham County Court
Nuneaton	Coventry County Court
Oswestry	Telford County Court
Oxford	Oxford County Court
Peterborough	Peterborough County Court
Pirehill North	Stoke-on-Trent County Court
Redditch	Worcester County Court
Rugby	Coventry County Court
Rugeley	Wolverhampton County Court
Rutland	Leicester County Court
Scunthorpe	Lincoln County Court
Seisdon	Wolverhampton County Court
Sleaford	Lincoln County Court
Shrewsbury	Telford County Court
Solihull	Birmingham County Court
South Herefordshire	Worcester County Court
South Warwickshire	Coventry County Court
Spilsby and Skegness	Lincoln County Court
Stoke-on-Trent	Stoke-on-Trent County Court
Stone	Stoke-on-Trent County Court
Stourbridge	Wolverhampton County Court
Sutton Coldfield	Birmingham County Court
Tamworth	Stoke-on-Trent County Court
Telford	Telford County Court
Toseland	Peterborough County Court
Towcester	Northampton County Court
Uttoxeter	Stoke-on-Trent County Court
Vale of Evesham	Worcester County Court
Warley	Wolverhampton County Court
Walsall	Wolverhampton County Court
Wellingborough	Northampton County Court
West Bromwich	Wolverhampton County Court
West Derbyshire	Derby County Court
Wisbech	Peterborough County Court
Witney	Oxford County Court
Wolds	Lincoln County Court
Wolverhampton	Wolverhampton County Court
Woodstock	Oxford County Court
Worcester City	Worcester County Court
Worksop	Nottingham County Court
	Northern Circuit
Appleby	Carlisle County Court
Ashton-under-Lyne	Manchester County Court
Barrow with Bootle	Lancaster County Court
Blackburn	Blackburn County Court
Blackpool	Lancaster County Court
Bolton	Manchester County Court

(i) Petty Sessions Areas	(ii) Care Centres
Burnley	Blackburn County Court
Bury	Manchester County Court
Carlisle	Carlisle County Court
Chorley	Blackburn County Court
Darwen	Blackburn County Court
Eccles	Manchester County Court
Fylde	Lancaster County Court
Hyndburn	Blackburn County Court
Kendal and Lonsdale	Lancaster County Court
Keswick	Carlisle County Court
Knowsley	Liverpool County Court
Lancaster	Lancaster County Court
Leigh	Manchester County Court
Liverpool	Liverpool County Court
Manchester	Manchester County Court
Middleton and Heywood	Manchester County Court
North Lonsdale	Lancaster County Court
North Sefton	Liverpool County Court
Oldham	Manchester County Court
Ormskirk	Liverpool County Court
Pendle	Blackburn County Court
Penrith and Alston	Carlisle County Court
Preston	Blackburn County Court
Ribble Valley	Blackburn County Court
Rochdale	Manchester County Court
Rossendale	Blackburn County Court
St Helens	Liverpool County Court
Salford	Manchester County Court
South Lakes	Lancaster County Court
South Ribble	Blackburn County Court
South Sefton	Liverpool County Court
South Tameside	Manchester County Court
Stockport	Manchester County Court
Trafford	Manchester County Court
West Allerdale	Carlisle County Court
Whitehaven	Carlisle County Court
Wigan	Liverpool County Court
Wigton	Carlisle County Court
Wirral	Liverpool County Court
Wyre	Lancaster County Court
	North Eastern Circuit
Bainton Beacon	Kingston-upon-Hull County Court
Barnsley	Sheffield County Court
Batley and Dewsbury	Leeds County Court
Berwick-upon-Tweed	Newcastle-upon-Tyne County Court
Beverley	Kingston-upon-Hull County Court
Blyth Valley	Newcastle-upon-Tyne County Court
Bradford	Leeds County Court
Brighouse	Leeds County Court
Calder	Leeds County Court
Chester-le-Street	Newcastle-upon-Tyne County Court
Claro	York County Court
Coquetdale	Newcastle-upon-Tyne County Court
Darlington	Teesside County Court
Derwentside	Newcastle-upon-Tyne County Court
Dickering	Kingston-upon-Hull County Court
Doncaster	Sheffield County Court
Durham	Newcastle-upon-Tyne County Court
Easington	Sunderland County Court
Easingwold	York County Court
Gateshead	Newcastle-upon-Tyne County Court
Hartlepool	Teesside County Court

(i) *Petty Sessions Areas*	*(ii)* *Care Centres*
Holme Beacon	Kingston-upon-Hull County Court
Houghton-le-Spring	Sunderland County Court
Howdenshire	Kingston-upon-Hull County Court
Huddersfield	Leeds County Court
Keighley	Leeds County Court
Kingston-upon-Hull	Kingston-upon-Hull County Court
Langbaurgh East	Teesside County Court
Leeds	Leeds County Court
Middle Holderness	Kingston-upon-Hull County Court
Morley	Leeds County Court
Morpeth Ward	Newcastle-upon-Tyne County Court
Newcastle-upon-Tyne	Newcastle-upon-Tyne County Court
Northallerton	Teesside County Court
North Holderness	Kingston-upon-Hull County Court
North Tyneside	Newcastle-upon-Tyne County Court
Pontefract	Leeds County Court
Pudsey and Otley	Leeds County Court
Richmond	Teesside County Court
Ripon Liberty	York County Court
Rotherham	Sheffield County Court
Ryedale	York County Court
Scarborough	York County Court
Sedgefield	Newcastle-upon-Tyne County Court
Selby	York County Court
Sheffield	Sheffield County Court
Skyrack and Wetherby	Leeds County Court
South Holderness	Kingston-upon-Hull County Court
South Hunsley Beacon	Kingston-upon-Hull County Court
South Tyneside	Sunderland County Court
Staincliffe	Leeds County Court
Sunderland	Sunderland County Court
Teesdale and Wear Valley	Newcastle-upon-Tyne County Court
Teesside	Teesside County Court
Todmorden	Leeds County Court
Tynedale	Newcastle-upon-Tyne Court
Wakefield	Leeds County Court
Wansbeck	Newcastle-upon-Tyne County Court
Whitby Strand	Teesside County Court
Wilton Beacon	Kingston-upon-Hull County Court
York	York County Court
	South Eastern Circuit
Ampthill	Luton County Court
Arundel	Brighton County Court
Ashford and Tenterden	Medway County Court
Aylesbury	Milton Keynes County Court
Barnet	Principal Registry of the Family Division
Barking and Dagenham	Principal Registry of the Family Division
Basildon	Chelmsford County Court
Battle and Rye	Brighton County Court
Beccles	Ipswich County Court
Bedford	Luton County Court
Bexhill	Brighton County Court
Bexley	Principal Registry of the Family Division
Biggleswade	Luton County Court
Bishop's Stortford	Watford County Court
Brent	Principal Registry of the Family Division
Brentwood	Chelmsford County Court
Brighton	Brighton County Court
Bromley	Principal Registry of the Family Division
Buckingham	Milton Keynes County Court
Burnham	Milton Keynes County Court
Cambridge	Peterborough County Court

(i) *Petty Sessions Areas*	*(ii)* *Care Centres*
Canterbury and St Augustine	Medway County Court
Chelmsford	Chelmsford County Court
Chertsey	Guildford County Court
Cheshunt	Watford County Court
Chichester and District	Brighton County Court
Chiltern	Milton Keynes County Court
Colchester	Chelmsford County Court
Crawley	Brighton County Court
Cromer	Norwich County Court
Crowborough	Brighton County Court
Croydon	Principal Registry of the Family Division
Dacorum	Watford County Court
Dartford	Medway County Court
Diss	Norwich County Court
Dorking	Guildford County Court
Dover and East Kent	Medway County Court
Downham Market	Norwich County Court
Dunmow	Chelmsford County Court
Dunstable	Luton County Court
Ealing	Principal Registry of the Family Division
Eastbourne	Brighton County Court
East Dereham	Norwich County Court
Ely	Peterborough County Court
Enfield	Principal Registry of the Family Division
Epping and Ongar	Chelmsford County Court
Epsom	Guildford County Court
Esher and Walton	Guildford County Court
Fakenham	Norwich County Court
Farnham	Guildford County Court
Faversham and Sittingbourne	Medway County Court
Felixstowe	Ipswich County Court
Folkestone and Hythe	Medway County Court
The Forest	Reading County Court
Freshwell and South Hinckford	Chelmsford County Court
Godstone	Guildford County Court
Guildford	Guildford County Court
Gravesham	Medway County Court
Great Yarmouth	Norwich County Court
Hailsham	Brighton County Court
Halstead and Hedingham	Chelmsford County Court
Harlow	Chelmsford County Court
Harrow Gore	Principal Registry of the Family Division
Haringey	Principal Registry of the Family Division
Harwich	Chelmsford County Court
Hastings	Brighton County Court
Havering	Principal Registry of the Family Division
Hertford and Ware	Watford County Court
Hillingdon	Principal Registry of the Family Division
Horsham	Brighton County Court
Hounslow	Principal Registry of the Family Division
Hove	Brighton County Court
Hunstanton	Norwich County Court
Huntingdon	Peterborough County Court
Ipswich	Ipswich County Court.
King's Lynn	Norwich County Court
Kingston-upon-Thames	Principal Registry of the Family Division
Leighton Buzzard	Luton County Court
Lewes	Brighton County Court
Lowestoft	Ipswich County Court
Luton	Luton County Court
Maidenhead	Reading County Court

(i) *Petty Sessions Areas*	*(ii)* *Care Centres*
Maidstone	Medway County Court
Maldon and Witham	Chelmsford County Court
Margate	Medway County Court
Medway	Medway County Court
Merton	Principal Registry of the Family Division
Mid-Hertfordshire	Watford County Court
Mid-Sussex	Brighton County Court
Mildenhall	Ipswich County Court
Milton Keynes	Milton Keynes County Court
Newham	Principal Registry of the Family Division
Newmarket	Ipswich County Court or Peterborough County Court
North Hertfordshire	Watford County Court
North Walsham	Norwich County Court
North Witchford	Peterborough County Court
Norwich	Norwich County Court
Peterborough	Peterborough County Court
Ramsgate	Medway County Court
Reading and Sonning	Reading County Court
Redbridge	Principal Registry of the Family Division
Reigate	Guildford County Court
Richmond-upon-Thames	Principal Registry of the Family Division
Risbridge	Ipswich County Court
Rochford and Southend-on-Sea	Chelmsford County Court
Saffron Walden	Chelmsford County Court
St Albans	Watford County Court
St Edmundsbury	Ipswich County Court
Saxmundham	Ipswich County Court
Sevenoaks	Medway County Court
Slough	Reading County Court
South Mimms	Watford County Court
Staines and Sunbury	Guildford County Court
Stevenage	Watford County Court
Steyning	Brighton County Court
Stow	Ipswich County Court
Sudbury and Cosford	Ipswich County Court
Sutton	Principal Registry of the Family Division
Swaffham	Norwich County Court
Tendring	Chelmsford County Court
Thetford	Norwich County Court
Thurrock	Chelmsford County Court
Tonbridge and Malling	Medway County Court
Toseland	Peterborough County Court
Tunbridge Wells and Cranbrook	Medway County Court
Waltham Forest	Principal Registry of the Family Division
Watford	Watford County Court
West Berkshire	Reading County Court
Windsor	Reading County Court
Wisbech	Peterborough County Court
Woking	Guildford County Court
Woodbridge	Ipswich County Court
Worthing	Brighton County Court
Wycombe	Milton Keynes County Court
Wymondham	Norwich County Court
	Wales and Chester Circuit
Ardudwy-is-Artro	Caernarfon/Llangefni County Court
Ardudwy-uwch-Artro	Caernarfon/Llangefni County Court
Bangor	Caernarfon/Llangefni County Court
Bedwellty	Newport (Gwent) County Court
Berwyn	Rhyl County Court
Brecon	Merthyr Tydfil County Court

(i) *Petty Sessions Areas*	*(ii)* *Care Centres*
Caernarfon and Gwyrfai	Caernarfon/Llangefni County Court
Cardiff	Cardiff County Court
Carmarthen North	Swansea County Court
Carmarthen South	Swansea County Court
Ceredigion Ganol	Swansea County Court
Chester	Chester County Court
Cleddau	Swansea County Court
Colwyn	Rhyl County Court
Congleton	Stoke-on-Trent County Court
Conwy and Llandudno	Caernarfon/Llangefni County Court
Crewe and Nantwich	Stoke-on-Trent County Court
Cynon Valley	Merthyr Tydfil County Court
De Ceredigion	Swansea County Court
Dinefwr	Swansea County Court
Dyffryn Clwyd	Rhyl County Court
East Gwent	Newport (Gwent) County Court
Eifionydd	Caernarfon/Llangefni County Court
Ellesmere Port and Neston	Chester County Court
Estimaner	Caernarfon/Llangefni County Court
Flint	Rhyl County Court
Gogledd Ceredigion	Swansea County Court
Gogledd Preseli	Swansea County Court
Halton	Warrington County Court
Hawarden	Rhyl County Court
Llandrindod Wells	Merthyr Tydfil County Court
Llanelli	Swansea County Court
Lliw Valley	Swansea County Court
Lower Rhymney Valley	Cardiff County Court
Macclesfield	Warrington County Court
Machynlleth	Merthyr Tydfil County Court
Merthyr Tydfil	Merthyr Tydfil County Court
Miskin	Merthyr Tydfil County Court
Mold	Rhyl County Court
Nant Conwy	Caernarfon/Llangefni County Court
Neath	Swansea County Court
Newcastle and Ogmore	Cardiff County Court
Newport	Newport (Gwent) County Court
Newton	Merthyr Tydfil County Court
North Anglesey	Caernarfon/Llangefni County Court
Penllyn	Caernarfon/Llangefni County Court
Port Talbot	Swansea County Court
Pwllheli	Caernarfon/Llangefni County Court
Rhuddlan	Rhyl County Court
South Anglesey	Caernarfon/Llangefni County Court
South Pembrokeshire	Swansea County Court
Swansea	Swansea County Court
Talybont	Caernarfon/Llangefni County Court
Upper Rhymney Valley	Merthyr Tydfil County Court
Vale of Glamorgan	Cardiff County Court
Vale Royal	Chester County Court
Warrington	Warrington County Court
Welshpool	Merthyr Tydfil County Court
Wrexham Maelor	Rhyl County Court
Ystradgynlais	Swansea County Court
	Western Circuit
Alton	Portsmouth County Court
Andover	Portsmouth County Court
Axminster	Taunton County Court
Barnstaple	Taunton County Court
Basingstoke	Portsmouth County Court
Bath and Wansdyke	Bristol County Court
Bideford and Great Torrington	Taunton County Court

(i) *Petty Sessions Areas*	*(ii)* *Care Centres*
Blandford and Sturminster	Bournemouth County Court
Bodmin	Truro County Court
Bournemouth	Bournemouth County Court
Bristol	Bristol County Court
Bridport	Bournemouth County Court
Cheltenham	Bristol County Court
Christchurch	Bournemouth County Court
Cirencester, Fairford and Tetbury	Bristol County Court
Cullompton	Taunton County Court
Dorchester	Bournemouth County Court
Droxford	Portsmouth County Court
Dunheved and Stratton	Truro County Court
Eastleigh	Portsmouth County Court
East Penwith	Truro County Court
East Powder	Truro County Court
Exeter	Plymouth County Court
Exmouth	Plymouth County Court
Falmouth and Kerrier	Truro County Court
Fareham	Portsmouth County Court
Forest of Dean	Bristol County Court
Gloucester	Bristol County Court
Gosport	Portsmouth County Court
Havant	Portsmouth County Court
Honiton	Taunton County Court
Hythe	Bournemouth County Court
Isle of Wight	Portsmouth County Court
Isles of Scilly	Truro County Court
Kennet	Bristol County Court
Kingsbridge	Plymouth County Court
Long Ashton	Bristol County Court
Lymington	Bournemouth County Court
Mendip	Taunton County Court
North Avon	Bristol County Court
North Cotswold	Bristol County Court
North Wiltshire	Bristol County Court
Odiham	Portsmouth County Court
Okehampton	Plymouth County Court
Penwith	Truro County Court
Petersfield	Portsmouth County Court
Plymouth	Plymouth County Court
Plympton	Plymouth County Court
Portsmouth	Portsmouth County Court
Poole	Bournemouth County Court
Pydar	Truro County Court
Ringwood	Bournemouth County Court
Romsey	Bournemouth County Court
Salisbury	Boumemouth County Court
Sedgemoor	Taunton County Court
Shaftesbury	Bournemouth County Court
Sherborne	Bournemouth County Court
Southampton	Portsmouth County Court
South East Cornwall	Plymouth County Court
South Gloucestershire	Bristol County Court
South Molton	Taunton County Court
South Somerset	Taunton County Court
Swindon	Bristol County Court
Taunton Deane	Taunton County Court
Tavistock	Plymouth County Court
Teignbridge	Plymouth County Court
Tewkesbury	Bristol County Court
Tiverton	Taunton County Court
Torbay	Plymouth County Court
Totnes	Plymouth County Court

(i) *Petty Sessions Areas*	*(ii)* *Care Centres*
Totton and New Forest	Bournemouth County C.ourt
Truro and South Powder	Truro County Court
Wareham and Swanage	Bournemouth County Court
West Somerset	Taunton County Court
Weston-Super-Mare	Bristol County Court
West Wiltshire	Bristol County Court
Weymouth and Portland	Bournemouth County Court
Wimborne	Bournemouth County Court
Winchester	Portsmouth County Court
Wonford	Plymouth County Court

(i) *London Commission Area*	*(ii)* *Care Centre*
Inner London Area and City of London	Principal Registry of the Family Division

EXPLANATORY NOTE

(This note is not part of the Order)

This Order provides for the allocation of certain proceedings concerning children between the High Court, the county courts and the magistrates' courts.

Article 3 prescribes certain proceedings which must be commenced in a magistrates' court.

Article 4 prescribes the court in which are to be brought applications to vary, extend or discharge orders.

Articles 5 to 13 regulate transfer between different courts and categories of court.

Articles 14 to 20, and Schedules 1 and 2, deal with the distribution of business amongst the county courts, and provide for the Principal Registry of the Family Division to be treated as a county court.

£3.00 net

ISBN 0 11 014677 8

Printed in the United Kingdom for HMSO

795 WO1443 C10 8/91 452 7102 O/N 134937

JOINT LORD CHANCELLOR' GUIDANCE/HOME OFFICE GUIDANCE (HOME OFFICE CIRCULAR NO 45/91)

THE CHILDREN (ALLOCATION OF PROCEEDINGS) ORDER 1991

1. The Lord Chancellor has power under Schedule 11 to the Children Act 1989 to provide for the commencement and transfer of proceedings in and between the High Court, county courts and magistrates' courts in specified circumstances. The Children (Allocation of Proceedings) Order 1991 has been made under that power with the intention of ensuring that cases under the Children Act and the Adoption Act 1976 should be directed to the most appropriate level of court.

2. The Children (Allocation of Proceedings) Order 1991 specifies that, in general, public law cases are to commence in the magistrates' court and, in addition, sets out the criteria by which such cases may be transferred either horizontally or vertically. The Order continues to allow applicants a free choice as to which court they commence private law proceedings but does allow for such proceedings to be transferred.

3. Proceedings under this Order will be heard in family proceedings courts as far as magistrates' courts are concerned. In county courts cases are allocated between divorce centres, family hearing centres and care centres. Cases which are heard in the High Court will be dealt with by the Family Division of that court. (An exception to this will be applications for secure accommodation (section 25) which are made in magistrates' courts but not to family proceedings courts).

Structure of the Order

4. Articles 1 and 2 provides for citation, commencement and interpretation of the Order and also for the classes of county courts. Articles 3 and 4 provides for commencement of proceedings. Articles 5 to 13 provides for the transfer of proceedings between courts. The allocation of proceedings to particular county courts is dealt with in articles 14 to 20. Article 21 covers the situation where a provision of the Order has not been complied with. There are three schedules to the Order: schedule 1 lists the divorce centres, schedule 2 lists the family hearing centres and schedule 3 links petty sessional areas with their respective county courts care centres.

COMMENCEMENT OF PROCEEDINGS

5. Article 3 provides that as a general rule all public law proceedings shall commence in a magistrates' court. This can be to any magistrates' court as there are no jurisdictional restrictions relating to magistrates' courts in this Order.

6. There are two exceptions to the general rule given in the above paragraph: a) where proceedings are brought following a section 37 direction made by the High Court or a county court; and b) where the article allows consolidation with certain pending public law proceedings. In the first situation such proceedings will be commenced in the court which made the direction where that court is the High Court or a county court care centre or in such county court care centre as the court which made the direction may order. In the second situation the proceedings should be commenced in the court where the other proceedings are pending.

7. As the Order does not specifically provide for the commencement of private law proceedings, such proceedings may be commenced in any level of court. However, if an applicant chooses to commence private law proceedings while a matrimonial cause relating to the child is pending in a particular county court, he must make his application to that court.

8. Article 4 requires that, in general, an application to vary, extend or discharge an order under the Children Act or the Adoption Act must be made to the court which made the original order. Such applications can be transferred if the criteria are satisfied. In contrast, applications for different orders shall be commenced like any other new application. For example, where an application for contact is made relating to a child who is the subject of a care order which was made by a county court, that application shall be made to a magistrates' court in accordance with article 3. But an application to discharge the care order would be made to the county court which made the original order.

Transfer of Proceedings

9. Articles 6 and 7 allow the transfer of proceedings from a magistrates' court to another court. The duties and powers given under those articles to magistrates' courts may be exercised by the court, a single justice or a justices' clerk.

Transfer from one magistrates' court to another

10. Article 6 allows magistrates' courts to transfer proceedings between themselves where it is in the interests of the child: a) because it will avoid delay; b) for the purposes of consolidation; or c) for some other reason. Before transfer to another magistrates' court may take place it is necessary for the receiving court's justices' clerk to consent to the transfer.

Transfer from a magistrates' court to a county court care centre

11. Article 7 only applies to public law proceedings and sets out the criteria for transfer of such proceedings from a magistrates' court to a county court. It provides for three criteria for transfer: a) exceptional gravity, importance or complexity; b) consolidation with pending proceedings; or c) urgency where no other magistrates' court can take the case. The first criterion of exceptional gravity, importance or complexity is expanded in the Order by the giving of particular examples.

12. Article 7 also lists those proceedings which are incapable of transfer including applications for emergency protection orders and applications associated with such orders, applications to protect children in an emergency under section 75 and contribution orders. Applications for secure accommodation orders (section 25) have restricted transferability as they may only be transferred if such an application is to be consolidated with other family proceedings.

13. Article 8 provides for the transfer of private law proceedings from a magistrates' court to a county court. The only criteria for such a transfer is that a magistrates' court considers that, in the interests of the child, the proceedings can be dealt with more appropriately in a county court. Such proceedings may be transferred to any divorce centre county court except where the proceedings are being transferred for reasons of consolidation. In that situation the case should be sent to where the other proceedings are pending.

Transfer from a magistrates' court to a county court following refusal of a magistrate's court to transfer public law proceedings

14. Where a magistrates' court has refused a party's request for public law proceedings to be transferred to a county court, article 9 permits an application to be made to the appropriate care centre county court, as given in schedule 3 to the Order, requesting that the proceedings be transferred. The district judge may grant this application where, on consideration of the criteria set out in article 7(l) (a) to (c), it considers a transfer to be in the interests of the child. The procedure for such applications is found in rule 4.6 in Part IV of the Family Proceedings Rules 1991.

Transfer from a county court to a magistrates' court

15. Article 11 allows a county court to return a public law case to the magistrates' court which transferred the case upwards but only if the case has not come to trial, (being that part of the proceedings where the issues of the case will be finally determined), and if certain conditions exist. These are that the criterion for transfer: a) does not apply where the criterion for transfer was exceptional gravity, importance or complexity; b) no longer applies in the case of a transfer for the purposes of consolidation because the proceedings in the county court have been determined; or c) no longer applies in the case of a transfer on the ground of urgency.

16. Before making an order for downward transfer the district judge must seek the views of the justices' clerk of the magistrates' court which sent the case upwards. Should the district judge, after considering those views, still decide to send the case back, he must give his reasons in writing. These requirements will appear in amendments to the Family Proceedings Rules. A party may appeal against the district judge's decision to a circuit judge.

Transfer from one county court to another county court

17. Article 10 allows county courts to transfer cases between themselves where this is in the interests of the child provided that either the receiving court has, or the presiding judicial officer at that court may exercise, the required jurisdiction. This article would, for example, permit a care case to be heard at an ordinary divorce centre provided that it was heard by a judge nominated by the Lord Chancellor to take care work.

Transfer from a county court to a High Court

18. Article 12 allows a county court to transfer any proceedings covered by the Order to the High Court where it considers that: a) the exceptional nature of the proceedings make them appropriate for determination there; and b) that such determination would be in the interests of the child.

Transfer from a High Court to a county court

19. Article 12 allows the High Court to transfer a case to a county court where the proceedings are appropriate for that court and it would be in the interests of the child.

Disapplication of enactments about transfer between county courts and the High Court

20. Article 5 disapplies sections 38 and 39 of the Matrimonial and Family Proceedings Act 1984 to proceedings under this Order. The reason for this is that this Order is now the appropriate place to provide for transfer of proceedings under the Children Act and Adoption Act between county courts and the High Court.

ALLOCATION OF PROCEEDINGS TO PARTICULAR COUNTY COURTS

21. Article 14 is the first of a series of articles which provide for the type of county court – ie divorce centre, family hearing centre or care centre – which may hear specific proceedings under the Acts covered by this Order. This article specifies that generally a private law application under the Children Act or the Adoption Act must be commenced in a divorce centre. This can be any divorce centre. As stated previously, there is one exception to this general rule – where a matrimonial cause is pending the application must be commenced in the court where that cause is pending.

Transfer of proceedings under Part I, II or Schedule 1

22. Articles 15 and 16 deal with the transfer of private law proceedings. Where a private law application is transferred from a magistrates' court to a county court it can be transferred to any divorce centre. The only exception to this is where a case is transferred for the purposes of consolidation. In those circumstances, the case will go to the court where the other proceedings are pending. Where a contested application for a section 8 order is being heard in a county court divorce centre which is not also a family hearing centre it must be transferred for trial to a family hearing centre. Where a private law application is transferred to a county court from the High Court it may be transferred to any divorce centre unless it is an application for a section 8 order in which case it must be transferred to a family hearing centre.

Application for adoption or freeing for adoption

23. Following the approach of article 16, a contested application for adoption or for freeing for adoption in a divorce centre which is not also a family hearing centre must be transferred for trial to a family hearing centre. Where an application under the Adoption Act is transferred to a county court from a magistrates' court, it may be transferred to any divorce centre.

Applications under Part III. IV or V

24. Article 18 provides that where a public law application is to be commenced in a county court, or to be transferred to a county court, that county court must be a care centre. In the case of a transfer from a magistrates' court, Schedule 3 lists the appropriate care centre to which the case should be transferred from any particular magistrates' court. This is the only occasion where the order requires a geographical link between transferring and receiving court.

Principal Registry of the Family Division

25. Article 19 makes the Principal Registry of the Family Division a divorce centre, a family hearing centre and a care centre. This ensures that the PRFD can take all cases under this Order.

Lambeth or Woolwich County Courts

26. Article 20 allows an application for a section 8 order or for an order under the Adoption Act to be commenced and tried in either the Lambeth or Woolwich County Courts.

Breach of any provision of the Order

27. Article 21 provides that no proceedings will be invalidated by the fact that those proceedings have been commenced or transferred in contravention of any provision of this Order.

Transitional Provision for Adoptions in County Courts

28. Article 22 is a transitional provision to ensure that adoption proceedings commenced in a county court before 14 October may remain in that court for trial. This article is needed because, at present, there is no requirement that adoption proceedings in a county court must be heard in a divorce county court.

Proceedings under Section 25

29. Where an application is made for a secure accommodation order during criminal proceedings, that application cannot be made to a family proceedings court and cannot be consolidated with family proceedings. This is in accordance with an amendment made to the Criminal Justices Bill.

FAMILY COURT COMMITTEE STRUCTURE

The Lord Chancellor's Department has established a committee structure to monitor the operation of the Children Act and to identify issues, mostly court-related, that arise from its implementation. Four levels of committee are involved: the Children Act Advisory Committee; the Annual Circuit Conferences; The Family Court Business Committees (FCBCs); and the Family Court Services Committees (FCSCs). They are not intended to form a hierarchy of committees, although reporting links have been established between the Children Act Advisory Committee and the other three levels of committee.

Each of the 51 Care centres will have an FCBC and an FCSC (apart from the Principal Registry of The Family Division, which has two FCBCs). Both the FCBCs and the FCSCs will be chaired by the Designated Family Judge and serviced by the Courts Administration.

The Children Act Advisory Committee

The terms of reference of the Advisory Committee are:

> *"to advise the Lord Chancellor, the Home Secretary, the Secretary of State for Health and the President of the Family Division on whether the guiding principles of the Children Act 1989 are being achieved and whether the court procedures and the guardian ad litem service are operating satisfactorily".*

The Circuit Conference

An annual one-day conference will be held on each Circuit (including the Principal Registry of the Family Division), to be chaired by the Family Division Liaison Judge. The purpose of the Conference is to provide a forum for inter-disciplinary discussion of issues relating to family proceedings. It is likely that issues raised at the FCSCs (see below) will provide a useful starting point for the conference agendas.

Family Court Business Committees (FCBCs)

The terms of reference for the FCBCs are as follows:

The Family Court Business Committee should:

(a) make sure that arrangements are working properly at local level, in particular allocation and transfer arrangements, meeting agreed targets where appropriate.

(b) seek to achieve administrative consistency between the two tiers of courts.

(c) ensure that the guardian ad litem and probation services are aware of the needs of the courts but avoid making unreasonable demands on those services.

(d) liaise with the area Family Court Services Committee.

Their membership is:–

Chairman – Designated Family Judge

Deputy Chairman – Courts Administrator

Members: District Judge
Representative of justices' clerks from courts operating family panels
Representative from local authority social services department
Representative from local authority legal department
Representative from a local Guardian Ad Litem panel

Local representative of the Legal Aid Board

Secretariat: Courts Administrator's Office

The membership of the FCBCs has been structured to provide representation from all the agencies whose management policies might affect the litigation process.

Family Court Services Committees (FCSCs)

The terms of reference for the FCSCs are as follows:

(a) to promote discussion and encourage co-operation between the professions, agencies and organisations involved in family proceedings;

(b) to consider and make recommendations for the resolution of problematical issues which arise in the conduct of family proceedings, with particular reference to the practice of:

- (i) the courts
- (ii) the legal profession
- (iii) the medical profession
- (iv) the health authorities
- (v) the social services
- (vi) the education authorities
- (vii) the police;

(c) to identify any necessary improvements to the service provided to the parties to family proceedings by the courts, or other agencies and professions.

(d) to liaise with the Family Court Business Committees.

Membership

In contrast to FCBCs - which have a small, fixed membership representing the main agencies involved in the litigation process - a more flexible approach is suggested for FCSC membership. The Lord Chancellor's Department have suggested 'core' membership of the committees as follows:

Core Membership

— Designated Family Judge (Chairman)
— a solicitor in private practice
— a solicitor from the local authority legal department
— a barrister
— a probation officer
— an area health authority representative
— a police representative
— a magistrate
— a justices' clerk
— a district judge
— at least one member of the medical profession, eg a child psychiatrist and/or a consultant in paediatrics
— a guardian ad litem (rather than a panel manager)
— a social workers
— Courts Administrator (Secretariat)

In addition, it is open to Courts Administrators, perhaps in discussion with the Designated Family Judge, to invite additional representatives according to local needs, interests, and problem areas and to invite individuals to attend particular meetings if an agenda item suggests it. The Lord Chancellor's Department has suggested the following additional possibilities for nomination, although these are not intended to be either mandatory or exclusive.

Suggested Additional Representation

- a health visitor
- a GP
- an education welfare officer
- an NSPCC representative
- voluntary groups
- a Citizens Advice Bureau representative
- a family law academic
- an education administrator or teacher.

Role of the FCBCs and FCSCs

FCBCs are concerned essentially with operational matters such as the mechanisms of the court process in handling children's cases. Their membership reflects the managerial ethos of those committees. The FCSCs, on the other hand, are composed of the professionals and the interest groups in the child care field. The sort of issues that they will be expected to discuss are those of a legal or welfare type, as well as matters of professional concern.

There may not always be a clear dividing line between the subject areas to be considered by the FCBCs and the FCSCs. The difference lies more in the approach to an issue that each committee should take. The FCBCs should be considering whether the framework laid down by the Act and the Rules of Court was working efficiently and within resource constraints, whereas the FCSCs may want to consider whether the framework has been correctly defined or whether other definitions should have been adopted. Either approach may lead to the identification of problems and suggestions for change, which is why the two kinds of committee are required to liaise with each other.

STATUTORY INSTRUMENTS

1991 No. 1924

LEGAL AID AND ADVICE, ENGLAND AND WALES

The Legal Aid Act 1988 (Children Act 1989) Order 1991

Made - - - -	*25th July 1991*
Laid before Parliament	*5th September 1991*
Coming into force	*14th October 1991*

The Lord Chancellor, in exercise of the powers conferred on him by sections 99(5), 104 of and paragraph 40 of Schedule 14 to the Children Act 1989(**a**), hereby makes the following Order—

Citation and commencement

1. This Order may be cited as the Legal Aid Act 1988 (Children Act 1989) Order 1991 and shall come into force on 14th October 1991.

Amendment of the Legal Aid Act 1988(b)

2. In section 15 of the Legal Aid Act 1988 (availability of, and payment for, representation under provisions relating to civil legal aid)—

(a) in subsection (1) for the words " (3B) " there shall be substituted " (3D) ";

(b) the following subsections shall be inserted after subsection (3B)—

" (3C) Subject to subsection (3A) but regardless of subsections (2) or (3), representation under this Part must be granted to the child in respect of whom the application is made, to any parent of such a child and to any person with parental responsibility for him within the meaning of the 1989 Act to cover proceedings relating to an application for the following orders under that Act—

(a) an order under section 31 (a care or supervision order);

(b) an order under section 43 (a child assessment order);

(c) an order under section 44 (an emergency protection order); or

(d) an order under section 45 (extension or discharge of an emergency protection order).

(3D) Subject to subsections (2) and (3), representation must be granted to cover proceedings relating to an appeal against an order made under section 31 of the 1989 Act to a person who has been granted representation by virtue of subsection (3C).

(3E) Subject to subsections (1) and (3A) but regardless of subsections (2) or (3), representation under this Part must be granted where a person applies to be or has been joined as a party to any of the proceedings mentioned in subsection (3C).".

Saving provisions

3. The provisions in Schedule 15 of the Children Act 1989 which repeal sections 27, 28, 30(1) and (2) of and paragraphs 2(a) and (e) of Part I of Schedule 2 to the Legal Aid Act 1988 shall apply only to applications for legal aid in respect of proceedings commenced on or after 14th October 1991.

Dated 25th July 1991 — *Mackay of Clashfern*,C

(**a**) 1989 c.41. (**b**) 1988 c.34

EXPLANATORY NOTE

(This note is not part of the Order)

This Order modifies the Legal Aid Act 1988:

(a) by waiving the means and merits tests in respect of applications for legal aid by a child, his parents and any person with parental responsibility for him in relation to proceedings under sections 31, 43, 44 and 45 of the Children Act 1989 (orders relating to the care and supervision, assessment or emergency protection of children) (the new section 15(3C));

(b) by waiving the means test for those parties mentioned in (a) above who are then parties to an appeal in relation to care proceedings (the new section 15(3D));

(c) by waiving the merits test in respect of other persons who apply to be or who are joined as parties to the proceedings specified in (a) above (the new section 15(3E)).

These provisions can be summarised as follows:

Proceedings	*Parties*	*Means/merits waived*	*Section*
section 31, 43, 44 and 45	child, parents, parental responsibility	means and merits	15(3C)
appeal of care proceedings	as above	means	15(3D)
application to join/joined as party to ss 31, 43, 44 and 45	any	merits	15(3E)

The existing provisions in the Legal Aid Act 1988 relating to the availability of legal aid for care proceedings and civil legal aid in magistrates' courts are preserved in relation to proceedings commenced prior to the Children Act 1989 coming into force.

60p net

ISBN 0 11 014924 6

Printed in the UK by HMSO
795/WO1682 C14 452/4 9/91 3212472 19542

1991 No. 2036

LEGAL AID AND ADVICE, ENGLAND AND WALES

The Civil Legal Aid (General) (Amendment) (No. 2) Regulations 1991

Made - - - -	*21st August 1991*
Laid before Parliament	*10th September 1991*
Coming into force	
regulation 20	*1st October 1991*
remainder	*14th October 1991*

The Lord Chancellor, in exercise of the powers conferred on him by sections 6(3), 15(3A), 16(6), 31, 34 and 43 of the Legal Aid Act 1988**(a)**, having had regard to the matters specified in section 34(9) and consulted the General Council of the Bar, the Law Society, and with the consent of the Treasury, hereby makes the following Regulations:

Citation, commencement and transitional provisions

1.—(1) These Regulations may be cited as the Civil Legal Aid (General) (Amendment) (No. 2) Regulations 1991.

(2) Regulation 20 shall come into force on 1st October 1991 and all other regulations shall come into force on 14th October 1991.

(3) Subject to paragraph (4), these Regulations shall apply to proceedings commenced on or after 14th October 1991 and the provisions of the Civil Legal Aid (General) Regulations 1989**(b)** shall apply in relation to proceedings commenced before that date as if these Regulations had not been made.

(4) Regulation 20 shall apply to any taxation carried out on or after 1st October 1991.

Interpretation

2. In these Regulations a regulation referred to by number means a regulation so numbered in the Civil Legal Aid (General) Regulations 1989.

Amendment of the Legal Aid Act 1988

3. After paragraph (b) of section 15(3A) of the Act there shall be inserted the word " or " and then the following new paragraph:—

"(c) to a guardian *ad litem*,"

Amendment of the Civil Legal Aid (General) Amendment Regulations 1989

4. In regulation 3—

(a) after the definition of " emergency certificate " there shall be inserted the following new definition:—

" family proceedings " has the meaning assigned by section 32 of the Matrimonial and Family Proceedings Act 1984**(c)**; ";

(a) 1988 c.34; section 15(3A) was inserted by the Children Act 1989 (c.41), section 99(2). Section 34 is amended by the Courts and Legal Services Act 1990 (c.41), Schedule 18, paragraph 63. Section 43 is an interpretation provision and is cited because of the meanings assigned to the words " prescribed " and " regulations ".
(b) S.I. 1989/339, as amended by S.I. 1991/524.
(c) 1984 c.42.

(b) the definition of "matrimonial proceedings" shall be omitted;

(c) after the definition of "patient" there shall be inserted the following new definition:—

"special Children Act proceedings" means proceedings under the Children Act 1989(**a**) for which representation must be granted to the applicant regardless of sections 15(1) to (3) of the Act;".

5. After regulation 3 there shall be inserted the following new regulation:—

"**Exclusion from civil legal aid of prescribed bodies**

3A. Representation under Part IV of the Act shall not be available to any body acting in a representative, fiduciary or official capacity for the purposes of proceedings under the Children Act 1989.".

6. At the beginning of regulation 12 there shall be inserted the words "Subject to regulation 12A,".

7. Regulations 12(2), 21(2), 45(3), 50(5), and 82(4) shall be omitted.

8. After regulation 12 there shall be inserted the following new regulation:—

"**Certificates relating to special Children Act proceedings**

12A.—(1) Where a person is entitled to legal aid for special Children Act proceedings, his solicitor shall lodge with the Area Director an application on a form approved by the Board at the first available opportunity and in any event within three working days of receiving instructions to act for that person in such proceedings.

(2) The application shall—

(a) state the name of the solicitor selected by the applicant to act for him; and

(b) contain a statement signed by the solicitor to the effect that legal aid is sought in respect of proceedings to which section 15(1) to (3) of the Act do not apply.

(3) Work done by a solicitor in relation to special Children Act proceedings prior to the issue of a certificate shall be deemed to be work done while such a certificate is in force provided that the application was lodged at the first available opportunity and in any event within the time specified in paragraph (1).".

9. At the beginning of regulation 18(1) there shall be inserted the words "Subject to section 15(3B) to (3D) of the Act and".

10. For regulation 28 there shall be substituted the following new regulation:—

"**Eligibility on the merits**

28.—(1) Without prejudice to the generality of sections 15(2) to (3C) and (3E) of the Act and subject to paragraph (2), an application for a certificate shall only be approved after the Area Director has considered all the questions of fact or law arising in the action, cause or matter to which the application relates and the circumstances in which the application was made.

(2) Where the application relates to proceedings to which section 15(3B), (3C) or (3E) of the Act apply, provided that the Area Director is satisfied that it does so relate and subject to regulation 27 (where applicable) he shall grant the application and Parts IV and V of these Regulations shall apply with any necessary modifications.".

11. In regulation 42 for the words "proceedings where an undertaking under regulation 12(2) has been given or" there shall be substituted "special Children Act proceedings or proceedings".

(**a**) 1989 c.41.

12. In regulation 46—

(a) At the beginning of paragraph (2) there shall be inserted the words " Except in the case of special Children Act proceedings ";

(b) For sub-paragraph (3)(a) there shall be substituted the following new sub-paragraph:—

"(a) family proceedings; or ";

(c) sub-paragraphs (3)(b) and (c) shall be omitted.

13. In regulation 47 for the words " matrimonial proceedings or authorised summary proceedings " there shall be substituted " family proceedings ".

14. At the beginning of regulation 76(3) there shall be inserted the words " Subject to section 15(3B) to (3D) of the Act,".

15. In regulation 94(d):—

(a) sub-paragraphs (iv) and (vii) shall be omitted;

(b) in sub-paragraph (vi) the words ", 11(2)(b) or (3)(b)" shall be omitted;

(c) in sub-paragraph (viii) for the words " section 34(1)(c) or 35 of the Children Act 1975 " there shall be substituted " the provisions of Schedule 1 to the Children Act 1989 ".

16. In regulation 96(1) the word " or " at the end of sub-paragraph (b) shall be omitted, there shall be inserted after " 1975 " in paragraph (c) " ; or " and at the end of that paragraph there shall be inserted the following new sub-paragraph:—

"(d) Schedule 1 to the Children Act 1989,".

17. In regulation 96(3)(b) and regulation 97(4) for the words " 12 per cent " there shall be substituted " 11 per cent ".

18. For regulation 104 there shall be substituted the following new regulation:—

" **Remuneration of legal representatives in magistrates' courts and family proceedings**

104.—(1) The sums to be allowed to legal representatives in connection with authorised summary proceedings shall be assessed by the Area Director.

(2) In the case of any family proceedings any assessment, review or taxation shall be made in accordance with the Legal Aid in Family Proceedings (Remuneration) Regulations 1991**(a)** and Part XII of these Regulations shall apply subject to the provisions of those Regulations.

(3) In the case of authorised summary proceedings which are not family proceedings any assessment, review or appeal under this regulation shall be made in accordance with the provisions of regulation 6 of and Schedule 1 Part I paragraph 1(1)(a) to the Legal Aid in Criminal and Care Proceedings (Costs) Regulations 1989**(b)** as if the work done was work to which these provisions apply, save that paragraphs 2 and 3 of Schedule 1, Part I shall not apply.

(4) Paragraphs (4) to (8) of regulation 105 and regulation 105A shall apply where costs are assessed by an Area Director under paragraph (1) as they apply to an assessment under that regulation.

(5) Subject to paragraph (4), regulations 105 to 110 shall not apply to costs in respect of authorised summary proceedings.".

19. After regulation 105 there shall be inserted the following new regulation—

" **Assisted person having financial interest in assessment**

105A.—(1) Where an assisted person has a financial interest in any assessment, review or appeal under this regulation he shall have a right to make written representations

(a) S.I. 1991/2038.
(b) S.I. 1989/343.

to the Area Director, appropriate area committee or committee appointed by the Board as the case may be within 21 days of being notified of the right to make such representations.

(2) On an assessment it shall be the duty of an assisted person's solicitor—

(a) to supply him with a copy of his bill;

(b) to inform him of any financial interest he may have in the assessment, the extent of any such interest and his right to make written representations; and

(c) to endorse on the bill whether or not the assisted person has a financial interest in the assessment and that he has complied with sub-paragraphs (a) and (b) above.

(3) Where a legal representative wishes to apply for a review of the assessment of the Area Director or appeal against a decision of the area committee under regulation 105 and the assisted person has exercised his right to make representations prior to the assessment, the legal representative shall notify him of the decision to be reviewed or appealed, the grounds of appeal and his right to make further written representations.".

20. In regulation 109—

(a) for paragraph (1) there shall be substituted the following new paragraph:—

109.—(1) Without prejudice to section 51(6) of the Supreme Court Act 1981**(a)**, Order 62, rules 10 and 11 of the Rules of the Supreme Court 1965**(b)** or to Order 38, rule 1(3) of the County Court Rules**(c)**, on any taxation of an assisted person's costs in connection with proceedings (which are not authorised summary proceedings) any wasted costs shall be disallowed or reduced, and where the solicitor has without good reason delayed putting in his bill for taxation the whole of the costs may be disallowed or reduced.";

(b) after paragraph (2) there shall be inserted the following new paragraph:—

"(3) In this regulation " wasted costs " has the same meaning as in section 51(7) of the Supreme Court Act 1981.".

21. For Regulation 119 there shall be substituted the following new regulation—

" **Assisted person having financial interest in taxation**

119.—(1) It shall be the duty of an assisted person's solicitor—

(a) to supply him with a copy of his bill;

(b) to inform him of any financial interest he may have in the taxation, the extent of any such interest and the steps which can be taken to safeguard that interest and, if the assisted person so requests, to give notice in accordance with rules of court to the taxing officer that the assisted person has such an interest; and

(c) to endorse on the bill whether or not the assisted person has a financial interest in the taxation and that he has complied with sub-paragraphs (a) and (b) above.

(2) Where the assisted person has a financial interest in the taxation he shall not be required to make any contribution to the fund on account of the costs of the taxation proceedings and the charge created by section 16(6) of the Act shall not apply in relation to any resulting increase in the net liability of the fund arising out of the costs of the taxation proceedings.".

25th July 1991 *Mackay of Clashfern*, C

We Consent,

Thomas Sackville
Sydney Chapman
Two of the Lords Commissioners
of Her Majesty's Treasury

21st August 1991

(a) 1981 c.54. Section 51(6) was substituted by section 4 of the Courts and Legal Services Act 1990 (c.41).
(b) S.I. 1965/1776; the relevant amending instrument is S.I. 1991/1884.
(c) S.I. 1981/1687; the relevant amending instrument is S.I. 1986/636.

EXPLANATORY NOTE

(This note is not part of the Regulations)

These Regulations amend the Civil Legal Aid (General) Regulations 1989, primarily to give effect to new procedures resulting from the Children Act 1989. In particular:

(1) guardians *ad litem* and any bodies acting in a representative, fiduciary or official capacity are excluded from representation for the purposes of the Children Act (regulations 3 and 5);

(2) effect is given to the amendments to section 15 of the Legal Aid Act 1988 (which waive either the means and merits requirements or just the merits requirements for certain parties to certain proceedings under the Children Act) (regulations 6, 8–11, and 14);

(3) the scope of legal aid certificates in relation to certain Children Act proceedings may extend to proceedings in the House of Lords or on appeal from a magistrates' court and may relate to more than one cause or matter and need not specify the parties to the proceedings in relation to proceedings under the Children Act (regulations 12 and 13);

(4) the £2,500 exemption from the statutory charge and the postponement of enforcement of the charge over money where it is to be used to purchase a home applies to proceedings under Schedule 1 to the Children Act (financial provision for children) (regulations 15 and 16);

(5) the rate of interest chargeable where enforcement of the statutory charge is postponed is reduced from 12% per annum to 11% (regulation 17);

(6) provision is made for the fees of legal representatives to be assessed in accordance with the provisions of the Legal Aid in Family Proceedings (Remuneration) Regulations 1991 (regulation 18);

(7) provision is made for an assisted person with a financial interest in the assessment to make written representations and for his solicitor to inform him of his rights, supply him with a copy of his bill and to endorse on the bill whether or not the assisted person has a financial interest and that he had complied with the other provisions (regulation 19) and corresponding amendments are made where the assisted person has a financial interest in taxation (regulation 21); and

(8) regulation 109 (which provides for the disallowance or reduction of costs due to fault on the part of the legal representative) is amended to bring it in line with the new provisions relating to costs against legal representatives under section 51(6) of the Supreme Court Act 1981 (regulation 20).

1991 No. 1925

LEGAL AID AND ADVICE, ENGLAND AND WALES

The Legal Aid in Criminal and Care Proceedings (General) (Amendment) (No.2) Regulations 1991

Made - - - -	*25th July 1991*
Laid before Parliament	*5th September 1991*
Coming into force	*14th October 1991*

The Lord Chancellor, in exercise of the powers conferred on him by sections 34 and 43 of the Legal Aid Act 1988**(a)**, hereby makes the following Regulations:–

Citation, commencement and transitional provisions

1.—(1) These Regulations may be cited as the Legal Aid in Criminal and Care Proceedings (General) (Amendment) (No.2) Regulations 1991 and shall come into force on 14th October 1991.

(2) These Regulations shall apply to proceedings commenced on or after 14 October 1991 and the provisions of the Legal Aid in Criminal and Care Proceedings (General) Regulations 1989**(b)** shall apply in relation to proceedings commenced before that date as if these Regulations had not been made.

Amendment of the Legal Aid in Criminal and Care Proceedings (General) Regulations 1989

2. Regulation 1(2) and Part VII of the Legal Aid in Criminal and Care Proceedings (General) Regulations 1989 shall be omitted.

3. In regulation 44(3) the words from "; and" in sub-paragraph (a) to "above" in sub-paragraph (b) shall be omitted.

Dated 25th July 1991 *Mackay of Clashfern, C.*

(a) 1988 c.34; section 34 was amended by the Courts and Legal Services Act 1990 (c.41), Schedule 18, paragraph 63. Section 43 is an interpretation provision and is cited because of the meaning assigned to the word "regulations". **(b)** S.I. 1989/344, as amended by S.I. 1990/489.

EXPLANATORY NOTE

(This note is not part of the Regulations)

These Regulations amend the Legal Aid in Criminal and Care Proceedings (General) Regulations 1989 by omitting the parts of the Regulations which refer to care proceedings (regulations 2 and 3). As a result of amendments to the Legal Aid Act 1988 by the Children Act 1989 (c.41) care proceedings now form part of civil legal aid. The unamended regulations are preserved to cover existing proceedings (regulation 1(2)).

60p net

ISBN 0 11 014925 4

Printed in the United Kingdom for HMSO

795 WO1680 C14 9/91 452 7102 O/N 134937

STATUTORY INSTRUMENTS

1991 No. 2037

LEGAL AID AND ADVICE, ENGLAND AND WALES

The Legal Aid in Criminal and Care Proceedings (Costs) (Amendment) (No. 3) Regulations 1991

Made - - - -	*21st August 1991*
Laid before Parliament	*10th September 1991*
Coming into force	*14th October 1991*

The Lord Chancellor, in exercise of the powers conferred on him by sections 34 and 43 of the Legal Aid Act 1988**(a)**, having had regard to the matters specified in section 34(9) and consulted the General Council of the Bar and the Law Society, and with the consent of the Treasury, hereby makes the following Regulations:—

1.—(1) These Regulations may be cited as the Legal Aid in Criminal and Care Proceedings (Costs) (Amendment) (No. 3) Regulations 1991 and shall come into force on 14th October 1991.

(2) These Regulations shall apply to the determination of costs which are payable in respect of work done on or after 14th October 1991 and costs payable in respect of work done before that date shall be determined as if these Regulations had not been made.

2. The following provisions of the Legal Aid in Criminal and Care Proceedings (Costs) Regulations 1989**(b)** shall be omitted—

(a) regulation 3(1)(d);

(b) regulation 6(5);

(c) the words " or care proceedings " in regulation 14(1)(a);

(d) paragraph 1(1)(b) of Part I of Schedule 1.

25th July 1991 *Mackay of Clashfern*, C.

We consent,

Thomas Sackville
Sydney Chapman
Two of the Lords Commissioners
of Her Majesty's Treasury

21st August 1991

(a) 1988 c.34; section 34 was amended by the Courts and Legal Services Act 1990 (c.41), Schedule 18, paragraph 63. Section 43 is an interpretation provision and is cited because of the meaning assigned to the word " regulations ".

(b) S.I. 1989/343, amended by S.I. 1990/488 and 1991/529 and 838.

EXPLANATORY NOTE

(This note is not part of the regulations)

These Regulations amend the Legal Aid in Criminal and Care Proceedings (Costs) Regulations 1989 by omitting thc provisions dealing with remuneration for care proceedings. [As a result of amendments to the Legal Aid Act 1988 by the Children Act 1989 (c.41), care proceedings after 14th October 1991 form part of civil legal aid. Provision for remuneration for care proceedings in all courts is now made in the Legal Aid in Family Proceedings (Remuneration) Regulations 1991 (S.I. 1991/2038).]

60p net

ISBN 0 11 015037 6

Printed in the UK by HMSO

795/WO1766 C16 452/4 9/91 3213134 19542

STATUTORY INSTRUMENTS

1991 No. 1881

CHILDREN AND YOUNG PERSONS

The Children Act 1989 (Consequential Amendment of Enactments) Order 1991

Made - - - -	*5th August 1991*
Laid before Parliament	*2nd September 1991*
Coming into force -	*14th October 1991*

The Lord Chancellor, in exercise of the powers conferred on him by section 108(9) of the Children Act 1989**(a)**, and of all other powers enabling him in that behalf, hereby makes the following Order:–

Citation and commencement

1. This Order may be cited as the Children Act 1989 (Consequential Amendment of Enactments) Order 1991 and shall come into force on 14th October 1991.

Child Benefit Act 1975(b)

2. Section 3(3)(c) of the Child Benefit Act 1975**(c)** (meaning of "person responsible for child") shall be amended by the insertion after the words "the National Health Service Act 1977" of the words ", the Children Act 1989".

Mental Health Act 1983(d)

3. Section 26(2) of the Mental Health Act 1983 (Definition of "relative" and "nearest relative") shall be amended by the substitution, for the words "his mother", of the following—

"(a) his mother, and

(b) if his father has parental responsibility for him within the meaning of section 3 of the Children Act 1989, his father.".

Local Government and Housing Act 1989(e)

4. Section 114(6) of the Local Government and Housing Act 1989 (Approval of applications to provide certain facilities for the disabled—meaning of "disabled") shall be amended by the omission of the word "or" immediately before paragraph (b) and by the insertion after that paragraph of the following:

"or

(c) a person to whom section 17(11) of the Children Act 1989 (disabled children) applies.".

(a) 1989 c. 41.
(b) 1975 c. 61.
(c) Section 3(3) has been amended by the National Health Service Act 1977 (c.49), Schedule 15, paragraph 67 and by the National Health Service (Scotland) Act 1978 (c.29), Schedule 15, paragraph 2.
(d) 1983 c.20.
(e) 1989 c.42.

5th August 1991 *Mackay of Clashfern,* C.

EXPLANATORY NOTE

(This note is not part of the Rules)

This Order makes amendments to statutory provisions in consequence of the Children Act 1989.

Article 2 amends section 3 of the Child Benefit Act 1975 (meaning of "person responsible for child") to add a reference to the Children Act 1989 under which, in addition to the enactments already there specified, residential accommodation will be provided for minors.

Article 3 amends section 26 of the Mental Health Act 1983 (Definition of "relative" and "nearest relative") to include in the definition of "relative" for the purposes of Part II of that Act (Compulsory admission to hospital and guardianship functions of relatives of patients) a father who has acquired parental responsibility for a child although he was not married to the child's mother at the time of the child's birth.

Article 4 amends section 114(6) of the Local Government and Housing Act 1989 (Approval of applications to provide, certain facilities for the disabled—meaning of disabled) to include a reference to those persons who are disabled children within the meaning of section 17(11) of the Children Act 1989.

60p net

ISBN 0 11 014881 9

Printed in the United Kingdom for HMSO

795 WO1638 C15 8/91 452/3 4235 134976 913320

THE CHILDREN (REPRESENTATIONS, PLACEMENTS AND REVIEWS) (MISCELLANEOUS AMENDMENTS) REGULATIONS 1991

This Statutory Instrument is made partly to correct errors in S.I. 1991/894 and 1991/890 and is being issued free of charge to all known recipients of these Statutory Instruments.

STATUTORY INSTRUMENTS

1991 No. 2033

CHILDREN AND YOUNG PERSONS

The Children (Representations, Placements and Reviews) (Miscellaneous Amendments) Regulations 1991

Made - - - -	*9th September 1991*
Laid before Parliament	*12th September 1991*
Coming into force	*14th October 1991*

The Secretary of State for Health in exercise of the powers conferred by sections 23(2)(a) and (f)(ii) and (5), 24(15), 26(5), 59(2), (3), and (5), and 104(4) of, and paragraphs 12(a), 13(a), and 14(a) of Schedule 2, paragraphs 4(1) and (2)(d) of Schedule 4, and paragraphs 7(1) and (2)(g) of Schedule 5, and paragraphs 10(1) and (2)(f) and (1) of Schedule 6, and paragraph 6 of Schedule 7 to the Children Act 1989**(a)**, and all other powers enabling him in that behalf, hereby makes the following Regulations:—

Citation and Commencement

1. These Regulations may be cited as the Children (Representations, Placements and Reviews) (Miscellaneous Amendments) Regulations 1991 and shall come into force on 14th October 1991 immediately after the regulations which they amend.

Amendments to the Representations Procedure (Children) Regulations 1991

2. The Representations Procedure (Children) Regulations 1991**(b)** shall be amended as follows—

(a) in regulation 4(2) (recording oral representations in writing), for the words from "agree that" to the end of the sentence, there shall be substituted the words "comment on the accuracy of the record.";

(b) after regulation 4(2), there shall be inserted the following paragraph—

> "(2A) The authority shall consider any comments made by the complainant under paragraph (2) and shall make any amendments to the record which they consider to be necessary.";

(c) for regulation 4(3) there shall be substituted—

> "(3) For the purposes of the following provisions of these Regulations, the written record referred to in paragraph (2), as amended where appropriate in accordance with paragraph (2A), shall be deemed to be the representations.";

(d) in regulation 9(3) (local authority consideration of what action to take), for the word "decisions" there shall be substituted "discussions";

(e) in regulation 12(2) (application of Regulations to representations by foster parents), for the words "Part I and III", there shall be substituted "Parts I to III".

(a) 1989 c.41. Section 24(14) and (15) were inserted by paragraph 9, and paragraph 14 of Schedule 2 was amended by paragraph 16, of Schedule 16 to the Courts and Legal Services Act 1990 (c.41).

(b) S.I. 1991/894.

Amendments to Arrangements for Placement of Children (General) Regulations 1991

3. The Arrangements for Placement of Children (General) Regulations 1991**(a)** shall be amended as follows—

(a) in regulation 5 (notification of arrangements)—

(i) paragraph (1)(e) shall be omitted;

(ii) in paragraph (1)(g), the words ", not being an officer of a local authority," shall be omitted.

Amendments to Review of Children's Cases Regulations 1991

4. After regulation 11 of the Review of Children's Cases Regulations 1991**(b)** there shall be inserted the following regulation—

"**Transitional Provisions**

12.—(1) Where immediately before 14th October 1991 a child is being accommodated by a local authority, a voluntary organisation or in a registered children's home, regulation 3 (time when each case is to be reviewed) shall have effect subject to the following provisions of this regulation.

(2) Where a child has been accommodated by a local authority, voluntary organisation or in a registered children's home for less than four weeks before 14th October 1991 and—

(a) there has not been a review of the case, that child's case shall be reviewed within four weeks of 14th October 1991 and thereafter in accordance with regulation 3(2);

(b) there has been a review of the case before 14th October 1991 that child's case shall be reviewed thereafter in accordance with regulation 3(2).

(3) Where a child has been accommodated by a local authority, voluntary organisation or in a registered children's home for four weeks or more, but for less than three months, before 14th October 1991 and—

(a) there has not been a review of the case, that child's case shall be reviewed within three months of 14th October 1991 and thereafter not more than six months after the date of the previous review;

(b) there has been a review of the case before 14th October 1991, that child's case shall be reviewed thereafter not more than six months after the date of the previous review.

(4) Where a child has been accommodated by a local authority, voluntary organisation or in a registered children's home for three months or more, but for less than six months, before 14th October 1991 and

(a) there has not been a review of the case, that child's case shall be reviewed within six months of the day on which the child was first so accommodated and thereafter not more than six months after the date of the previous review;

(b) there has been a review of the case by 14th October 1991 that child's case shall be reviewed thereafter not more than six months after the date of the previous review.

(5) Where a child has been accommodated in a registered children's home otherwise than by a local authority or voluntary organisation for more than 6 months before 14th October 1991 that child's case shall be reviewed within 6 months of 14th October 1991 and thereafter not more than 6 months after the date of the previous review.".

Signed by authority of the Secretary of State for Health

Virginia Bottomley
Minister of State,
Department of Health

9th September 1991

(a) S.I. 1991/890.
(b) S.I. 1991/895.

EXPLANATORY NOTE

(This note is not part of the Regulations)

These Regulations make minor amendments to regulations 4, 9 and 12 of the Representations Procedure (Children) Regulations 1991 and regulation 5 of the Arrangements for Placement of Children (General) Regulations 1991 (notification of arrangements) (regulations 2 and 3).

They also add transitional provisions to the Review of Children's Cases Regulations 1991, relating to the time at which the cases of specified children who are accommodated before 14th October 1991 are to be reviewed (regulation 4).

AMENDMENTS TO CHILDREN ACT REGULATIONS

The Children (Representations, Placements and Reviews) (Miscellaneous Amendments) Regulations 1991 provide for the following amendments to the Representations Procedure (Children) Regulations 1991 and the Arrangements for Placement of Children (General) Regulations 1991:

Representations Procedure (Children) Regulations 1991

Regulations 4 and 9 have been amended to clarify that a complainant who makes an oral complaint which the local authority records in writing is given the opportunity to comment on that written record.

Arrangements for Placement of Children (General) Regulations 1991

Regulation 5 is amended by the new Regulations to require the local authority to include among those notified of the arrangements to place a child, an officer of the local authority who was caring for the child other than in a professional capacity immediately before the arrangements were made. Under the original Regulation, such an officer of the local authority was excluded from notification. This amendment also removes an unintentional duplication in the list of those who should be notified (Regulation 5(e) and (f) referred to the same authority).

Printed in the United Kingdom for HMSO.
Dd.0295238, 10/91, C280, 3385/4, 5673, 167919.